ADOLESCENCE:
HOW TO SURVIVE IT

ADOLESCENCE: HOW TO SURVIVE IT

Insights for Parents,
Teachers and Young Adults

TONY LITTLE
AND HERB ETKIN

BLOOMSBURY CONTINUUM
LONDON · OXFORD · NEW YORK · NEW DELHI · SYDNEY

BLOOMSBURY CONTINUUM
Bloomsbury Publishing Plc
50 Bedford Square, London, WC1B 3DP, UK

First published in Great Britain 2019

A catalogue record for this book is available from the British Library

Library of Congress Cataloguing-in-Publication data has been applied for

ISBN: HB: 978-1-4729-4470-2; ePDF: 978-1-4729-4468-9;
ePub: 978-1-4729-4471-9

2 4 6 8 10 9 7 5 3 1

Typeset by Deanta Global Publishing Services, Chennai, India
Printed and bound in Great Britain by CPI Group (UK) Ltd, Croydon CR0 4YY

To find out more about our authors and books visit www.bloomsbury.com
and sign up for our newsletters

CONTENTS

AUTHORS' NOTE

TONY LITTLE

My own adolescence was much like any other. By turns blasé and enthusiastic, surly and outgoing, brashly confident and insecure, I had all the bewildering uncertainties and pipe dreams of a typical teenager. Of only one thing was I sure as I looked to the future: that I would never become a teacher.

My family had little history of formal education: the notion of sixth form, let alone university, was wholly alien. If you were lucky enough to have the chance of a good education, that was the route to a better life on an elevated plane, a way up and out. Becoming a teacher didn't fit that vision at all. My father, who left school at 14, said it was a waste of a good opportunity.

I drifted into teaching, as many do. Indeed, some of the best teachers I have known only discovered their vocation on the job after uncertain beginnings. In my case, I developed a growing fascination with the contradictions in front of me: creatures both frustrating and compelling. My wife was an excellent teacher of younger children. I couldn't do that. Somehow I felt more at home with teenage swirls of uncertainty. Their quests for identity and their attempts to make sense of relationships initially seemed like spectres at the feast in my classroom. I always seemed to have to adjust my English teaching to the dynamics of a particular group or an individual's issues. Only later did I realize that this was the point: these things were the feast.

I moved from the classroom to headship, and there had to confront the bigger picture. Plenty of people I met, parents and teachers, treated adolescence as an aberration, a period to be got through as best as one can, before recognizable, mature life begins. It was then I became more aware of just what an exciting time adolescence is: the path pitted with risks and traps, but also with a marvellous appetite to experience new things and an openness that's inspiring. A hugely distinguished television producer told me that every one of his new ideas (which had subsequently been internationally successful) had been initially dismissed as crazy by adults: it was only the 15-year-olds who saw the potential.

For over a quarter of a century I was a head of three British independent schools. Fee-paying schools are privileged places, though rather more diverse these days than some people think. Yet adolescence can be a tricky time, including for those who appear to have all the material comforts they might need. I've enjoyed close ties with a number of British state schools and have also been responsible for schools around the world, from Shanghai to Kampala, from rural India to urban Europe. It's notable that adolescent problems tend to feature more strongly in more developed societies (there's little time for them when wage-earning to survive starts young), but what really strikes me is that the underlying issues are broadly similar. Adolescence is an essential part of the human condition.

I got by in my career in schools by trying to exercise a degree of common sense and a dash of humanity. If I'm honest, I've been sceptical about our contemporary fetish for over-analysing and medicalizing pretty much anything to do with adolescence, but I want to find out more from a real expert in adolescent psychology and behaviour. What have I been missing?

HERB ETKIN

I had never envisaged a career other than medicine, or so I am unreliably informed by my family. I grew up in South Africa, so sport was an essential part of daily life, greatly enjoyed but undistinguished as far as I was concerned. The rest of my adolescence was conventional and unremarkable.

After qualifying in medicine in Johannesburg, and additional training in paediatrics, I became a partner in a semi-rural general practice on South Africa's Natal coast, where my family spent several happy years. My experience in general practice made it obvious to me that much of the daily caseload included psychiatric and psychological problems. After some hesitation and discussion, as I had never considered specializing, we moved to Johannesburg where I trained as a psychiatrist.

Having three daughters was an undoubted factor in my burgeoning interest in the problems of young people. As a consequence of this I chose to leave my fulfilling post as university lecturer and consultant at an adult hospital to move to Britain, where proper training in that field was available. I was appointed Senior Registrar at a new adolescent psychiatric unit, and sat the first ever Royal College of Psychiatrists examination.

After a short return to South Africa, I came back to a permanent consultant post covering Brighton and the south-east of England. At that time, South Africa was still flourishing economically (if not politically), whilst Britain was in the grip of political and financial difficulties. We were referred to as the first ever case of rats fleeing *onto* the sinking ship!

Nevertheless, we loved living in the country with which so many of my generation had identified: that of Biggles, *Just William*, Enid Blyton, cricket, top-class football and so many cultural opportunities even in the most unlikely settings.

Important, too, was the excellent way in which services for families and children at that time were provided under the Child Guidance system. Full therapeutic teams were available for rapid responses, but problems were nowhere near as extensive as they are for the NHS's overloaded CAMHS (Child and Adolescent Mental Health Services), as they are named nowadays. Referral rates are rocketing, with insufficient resources, reduced in-patient facilities and poor recruitment of essential professionals. An inability to respond rapidly to urgent situations has led to many tragic outcomes.

Sadly, after about 5 years in the UK, my wife and I parted. This necessitated a crash course in the 'mothering' of teenage daughters while working full-time. Not recommended! My second wife, Jane, is a much valued, adored and appreciated addition to the family, which now includes nine grandchildren.

INTRODUCTION

In this book we have set out to provide a straightforward source of information, advice, and perhaps even comfort, to all those who come into contact with young people at critical periods of their intertwining lives. It is not designed to be a tome for experienced professionals working with those in trouble. Both of us have careers, as psychiatrist and schoolmaster, which have revolved around young people and their families in either 'normal' or difficult circumstances. No two situations are the same, and inevitably gender, cultural, ethical and social differences come into play.

References to academic studies and other texts will therefore be provided rarely, but inevitably almost everything in the book stems not just from our own experiences but the innumerable commentators and writers who throughout history have had much to say about the process of adolescence, and the way in which it has impacted on them personally and on all those around them. It is part of the essential rhythm of life that adolescents should at various stages test what is going on around them – and what better place to start than within the family? This is seldom a rational and considered process: more often than not there is upset and anger along the way, and sometimes even hate on both sides.

Adolescence is a time of great change, and that change can be made manifest in a variety of ways. An adolescent boy may be bigger and stronger than his father, or better educated, or even earn more than older members of his family. It can be an unsettling time, and recourse to the phrase 'in my day' is a common, defensive reaction; it is also unhelpful, given that society is changing at a dramatic pace. We all develop in stages, often overlapping, continually changing according to both internal and external influences. Physical, sexual, emotional and intellectual burgeonings are compounded by changes in the nuclear family, the extended family and society at large. The starting point matters, too: inevitably, the way in which adolescence unfolds is greatly dependent on the experiences of the childhood that has formed the foundation for this period of development.

The way we interpret new experiences and react to them can largely be attributed to what has gone on in our minds in earlier life, both within the home and elsewhere. In this book, we look at how things develop in the home, how they develop in school, how they develop with peers and how they relate to the outside world. Many developmental theorists believe that to grow into a coherent and acceptable adult, it is essential to go through a questioning and critical phase, challenging the adult world and all the facets of its functioning. This is the 'independence phase', which can only be formed by questioning and re-interpreting. Rebelliousness is part of this process, as adolescents feel in conflict with the society around them, largely because they are unsure about what they see and feel. During this period, the adolescent is open to different information and alternative 'truths', and can also become controlled by thoughts or philosophies that are not easy to displace in later life. He or she can even develop prejudices and hatreds that can become deeply ingrained, and nurtured by those with whom they then seek to associate, be it street gangs or religious groups. Anna Freud describes the whole process as a 'normal psychosis'.

For the family, all is not lost, even though it can sometimes feel like it. As long as adults do what they are supposed to do – playing by reliable rules and acting as fixed points on the landscape – young people, on the whole, feel safe and secure. In the long term most will grow up to be like mum and dad –culturally, emotionally and philosophically similar in their own parental actions in turn. At the same time, they will wish to see themselves as individuals: as confident, reasonably assertive human beings who have become independent.

But there is a powerful new complicating factor. Many of the concepts of early theorists such as Freud, Bowlby and Erikson have been greatly distorted by the fast-developing electronic age in which we live. Television, internet and social media have too often taken pseudo-parental roles of great influence with many children. Even the very young child who has frequently been plonked down in front of a television has been exposed to a deep and lasting influence – and that is long before the effects of social media have been brought to bear.

In a perplexing world we tend to turn to the experts. However, different schools of earlier theorists have not agreed about much. In addition to this confusion, a great deal has been written in books and articles by other 'experts' expressing personal views and advice relating to narrow social norms within their own experience. Most of this is now out-of-date: has disappeared as everything in our lives changes at an ever-faster pace, with the arrival of instant electronic information, communication overload and undetected invasions of privacy.

We now know more, particularly with the advent of neuroscience. The notion that personality is fixed between the age of three and five is now shown to be false: our personalities develop throughout our lives. We know that the tightly defined age parameters of adolescence have been proven to be wrong: adolescence goes on a lot longer than we thought, well into the 20s. We know that lifetime trajectories are not certainties, but fragile advances susceptible to shift and change. Most importantly, we know that adolescence is not just an irritating period to be got over with as quickly as possible, but a time of crucial creativity and inventiveness that should be nurtured and celebrated.

Some themes, however, have stood the test of time. In 1908, Van Gennep coined the phrase 'rites of passage', thus giving shape to an idea that has been the subject of many studies over the last century. The importance of the central idea has become well-defined. Overt rituals that clearly define the transition from child to adult have largely been discarded by modern societies, but were an important part of primitive societies throughout history. Some recent studies point to a lack of these rituals as being a contributory factor in violence, delinquency and substance abuse. Looked at another way, rituals have found new clothing. There are, for example, strong similarities between the context of a street gang and a boarding school: while the behaviour of these two groups may be dramatically different, both groups create a strong, positive culture of support, like a family.

As a society, we compound the pressure on adolescents by relating the milestones on the road to adulthood by chronological age, and not maturity or the ability to function effectively. Voting, driving, joining the army are all transitions young people associate with perceptions of being grown-up, just as, further down the line, marriage, parenthood and owning a property provide other moments of transition. Chronological age and developmental age, physical and psychological, are frequently out of kilter.

The urge to seek clarity in the muddy waters of adolescence is further compounded by changes in society. The millennial generation, for example, settles down later, remains more dependent on family for longer, and leaves home later than past generations.

That road to adulthood can be long and winding. Whereas puberty is a physical process occurring in all children at similar times, according to nutrition, weight and external factors, adolescence is an evolved process in developed societies.

Adolescence is a tricky thing: it is a crucial part of the human experience, but it can affect everyone in different ways. For this psychiatrist and schoolmaster, our shared fascination in this apparently strange period of human development has led to many conversations.

It could be said that a normal adolescent is just somebody who has yet to be fully investigated.

This is what we seek to do.

1

Adolescence: What Is It?

Adolescence is not an incurable disease. Every one of us has gone through this process, but this by no means ensures we have a good understanding of how anyone else has experienced it – even our own children, let alone those going through it at the moment or who will soon do so.

First, a definition. Adolescence is a bridge between childhood and adulthood, is of varying length, and is filled with all sorts of possibilities, dangers, enjoyments, pleasures and, above all else, the excitement of discovery. The trouble is that 'adolescence' is open to all kinds of interpretation. It will often be experienced by the individuals themselves very differently from the way their parents or families view it, or their teachers, or their peer groups or anyone else who comes into contact with them. It is a variable process, in which the young people concerned have to learn to detach from parents and family (and vice versa), whether they want to or not, and function in a way that is true to their own personality. But personality itself is subject to influences from all quarters, be they peer groups, idols, the internet, genetics . . . It is a long list. However hard parents may try to deny it, influences outside the home, and other safe structures like school, are hugely important, and children have to cope with them.

A challenge for all of us is that there are few fixed points in adolescence – one of the reasons why there are different interpretations of it in the expert world. What is central, however, is the essential break between child and parents, and the first step upon the road to true independence or an independent lifestyle. Teenage questioning is a healthy development, though it can take many forms. Young people need to test out a myriad of behaviours and attitudes. When this happens in the relative safety of their own homes, parents can share the experience, analysing it with or without the child present, and perhaps help change what at first appears an inevitable pathway. If a teenager is able to bring some shared family values to bear, he or she will end up as a stronger, more flexible individual with a higher self-esteem, and be more able to go into the world as a confident adult. Parents should not allow family values to be denigrated, demeaned and disposed of. Yet at the same time it is right that some family values be held up to the light by a teenager, scrutinized and found wanting.

This teenage scrutiny can sometimes be a painful experience, but there is a shared humanity in the awareness that all human beings have their limitations. Just as teachers have to learn to recognize that some students are more intellectually able than them, so parents have to accept that a teenager's view has validity. Parents and teachers need to take the 'long view'. The family values that parents regard as central to a life well lived are not necessarily accepted by the adolescent in their entirety, but they may well be infused over a period of time, perhaps long after the teenager has left home. Yet for both the teenager and the family, there has to be acceptance that certain values are obtained in peer-group relationships and elsewhere. These values relate to thinking about others, having compassion, empathy and an awareness that one can still learn without words being said. Responding to people in a nuanced, multi-faceted way is crucial to teenagers' future development.

They need to learn, too, that not everyone thinks the way they do; and that it is very common to make a mistake, not least by projecting personal views onto somebody else and wondering why the reaction is the opposite of that anticipated. Witnessing this sometimes torturous process of awakening can be frustrating, and a real challenge for parents. It can feel pretty tortured to their children, too.

Adolescence is commonly associated with teenagers. In practice, adolescence is a moving feast, and can kick in well before the age of 13 and certainly extend well beyond the teenage period, particularly in the case of boys; girls tend to mature earlier. One piece of recent research identifies the terminal point of male adolescence as late as the age of 28. When it comes to risk-taking, an awareness that men in their 20s are still 'adolescent' may help explain something about young adult behaviour, from laddish posturing to warfare.

Studies of brain development have enabled us to see the significance of the frontal lobe in emotional development, in the creation of effective controls and decision-making around ethics and morality. They show that this process can run for at least a decade. In most cases, a virtuous circle is set up as the acquisition of skills and employment leads to feelings of self-worth and esteem, which in turn mark the path to balanced independence. There are good ways to guide people along the way: for example, the Scouts and Guides in the West and the Young Pioneers in Russia offer a process of transition enabling young people to gain acceptance and understanding of responsibilities, empathy and social behaviours, including altruism. Some religious programmes, such as baptisms, confirmations and bar mitzvahs, have played and continue to play a key role. The American organization Rope (Rights of Passage Experience) engages with young people to help them understand the importance of healthy decisions in sexual relationships in the workplace, in play and so on.

WHO IS AFFECTED?

Tony: Herb, from your professional experience, who is affected?

Herb: We all are. Whether or not we are going through adolescence ourselves, it's an experience we all have, both as individuals and as part of a social group, especially the family.

Tony: We know that no two adolescent experiences are the same, even for identical twins. How, then, can one hope to have any kind of uniform approach to such a diverse and complex business? It seems pretty amazing that anyone could be normal. Given the range of young people who have had to deal with it over the years, is it possible even to talk about such a thing as normal?

Herb: Adolescence is certainly complex, but in a society that seems to change at the most alarming speed, it's more challenging than ever before. It's a wonder that anyone emerges to be relatively normal at the end of it.

Tony: Are you saying there is no such thing as 'normal' in adolescence?

Herb: There is a wide perception of 'normality' that refers to all aspects of growth and development in young people, but it's a subjective and imprecise thing.

Tony: What would you describe as a broad normality?

Herb: Adolescence has morphed and continues to evolve at an astonishing rate, reflecting the wider changes in life around us. The common theme is that adolescence is a personal experience, and parents have to learn to accept that their children do not necessarily behave in the way they did – or (more likely) imagine they did.

Tony: So what really has changed? Surely the human condition is constant?

Herb: When it comes to academic discussion of adolescence, it frequently seems nothing has really altered, but that's far from the truth, because modern families and children have a kaleidoscope of change around them. As we enter an era of exponential advances, driven by artificial intelligence, the experiences and possibilities facing teenagers will be utterly different from those their parents might have experienced.

Tony: Which means an understanding of adolescence is more important than ever before?

Herb: Undoubtedly, especially now that the small screen is such a powerful and seemingly unstoppable force as a comforter, informer and, potentially, destroyer. It's a loaded weapon for friend and foe.

Tony: I see potential for harm at the other end of the scale. Too many young people are not taught or allowed to be adventurous, to learn how to keep themselves safe and sort out problems for themselves. Over-attentive parents can cause as much damage as unfettered access to the small screen. Schools can compound the problem: the increasing threat of litigation over all manner of things can cause whole institutions to become risk-averse. There's a balance to be struck, hard though that can be.

Herb: It's the imbalance that causes the problems. Whether children are spoon-fed or neglected by school or parents, there is a blurring of roles, particularly around the response to authority and morality, which can lead to feelings of hopelessness, helplessness and haplessness – all three in some young people, very little in others. If these feelings are profoundly felt, trouble will arise.

Tony: What can make it complicated for parents is that adolescence doesn't just suddenly start up at specific times, unlike periods for girls. It's clear that powerful influences impact significantly on the way adolescence unfolds: genetics, siblings, experience at nursery and junior school, and many others. All these influences prepare the ground for long-term lifestyle patterns, much of which happens during the phase we call *adolescence*. It's one of the most crucial and fascinating phases of our lives.

2

Rites of Passage

The shifting sands of youthful behaviour have been seen as treacherous by adults for many centuries. Indeed, antiquity seems littered with references to the failings of the young. A Babylonian clay pot, some 3,000 years old, bemoans the rottenness of youth and that young people are not what they were. In his *Rhetoric*, Aristotle told his audience about the fickle and unpredictable nature of youth: impulsive, irascible and impassioned, with little capacity to delay gratification or to tolerate criticism. These historic references come from well-established, civilized societies. Perhaps Socrates is their spokesman: 'Our youth now love luxury. They have bad manners, contempt for authority; they show disrespect for their elders and love chatter in place of exercise; they no longer rise when elders enter their room; they contradict their parents, chatter before company, gobble up their food and tyrannize their teachers'. Some might say, *plus ca change*!

In more primitive societies where life was much shorter and more difficult, it was less easy to give children a special, extended period in which to grow and learn about all sorts of things. In a limited and constrained society, there is no social need for the period we call adolescence. In such societies young people are trained within specific parameters to perform the same functions lifelong. Nonetheless, this special period was recognized. In the early 11th century the Anglo-Saxon monk Byrhtferth drew up a manual documenting scientific knowledge. A central belief was that the elements and seasons were reflected in mankind. Thus, the same diagram that shows Spring–Summer–Autumn–Winter also illustrates Childhood (Pueritia), Adolescence (Adolescentia), Youth (Juuentas) and Old Age (Senectus).

In a world of opportunity, change and diversity, however, adolescence becomes pivotal. It is the period during which young people come to terms with a huge range of opportunities in their later lives. It is the means by which they are able to navigate a complex adult world which has vast horizons. In that sense, adolescence is a phenomenon of a civilized culture.

But even that definition risks being simplistic. There can be subcultures within a society that seek to predetermine the life experiences of young people, in which case adolescence can come to be seen as self-indulgence. This can create tensions for young people as they grow up. Adolescence should be a good and healthy thing. If suppressed it can cause problems for teenagers and adults alike. In most societies and through much of history, however, adolescence has been treated as a social aberration. Societies have demanded young adults as soon as possible. In times past, survival in a hostile environment permitted just two groupings: adults and children; there was no middle ground. Yet through most societies there is a linking thread: a belief in rites of passage.

RITES OF PASSAGE

Tony: Progressing from one group to another, from childhood to adulthood, has often been marked by some kind of formal process. The phrase 'rites of passage' is well established in the language and literature of the West, even if sometimes presented in a nuanced or ironic way. Such a rite seems to have been practised more straightforwardly in other parts of the world.

Herb: It certainly isn't a new phrase. Indeed, it's been around for over a century, and has been widely studied by social anthropologists in more primitive societies. Traditional African rites of passage, for example, are quite straightforward: the key milestones are birth, adulthood (somewhere around the age of 12 or 13), marriage, eldership and ancestorship. Adolescence doesn't feature specifically. As a social development rather than a physical state, it's dealt with differently.

Tony: Tribes and communities around the world have developed their own clearly articulated and readily understood rites of passage, from the Aboriginal walkabout, the Maasai lion hunt and Native Americans fasting in the wild, to circumcisions, tattoos, teeth-sharpening, scarification and so on. I remember you telling me once that in its most extreme form in Papua New Guinea, the Sambian culture of purification required boys to leave home for ten years from the age of seven, and involved nose bleeding, forced vomiting and even semen ingestion in order to become a man. This all sounds bizarrely dramatic: I wonder whether in the West we have sublimated these innate, raw human instincts, or whether it's just a reflection of different societies having different needs.

Herb: If one looks at these rituals in the whole, there tends to be a process that is quite logical: separation, instruction, transition and finally a welcome back to the community. Most primitive societies' rites of passage were clear-cut, and in those remaining societies that still practise them, life for young people can be very much easier than in the West. Western culture is an ever-moving feast: we view life differently from the way we did even 30 years ago, let alone a hundred years.

When it comes to clearly defined rites, young people in primitive societies know what to expect, when to expect it and how to practise what they have been taught. In traditional tribal communities they are subjected to initiation processes and ceremonies which focus on how to be acceptable adults, understanding the rules, regulations and prevailing morality, including what is expected of them regarding sexual behaviour. The ceremonies are undertaken at specific periods, clearly set out for both boys and girls.

Tony: So they can conform without having the unrealistic expectations so evident in developed societies. That sounds rather wonderful, but this push for conformity could sometimes be punitive, so ritual has not always been a force for good. Female genital mutilation, for example, is very damaging to the individuals involved both emotionally and physically, and still continues. This is a type of conformity that seems not unlike branding cattle or sheep, marking out young people as belonging to a particular owner or tribe.

Herb: That's true, but in the West the impact is more strongly felt in, if you like, a lack of conformity, or at least a lack of clearly identified rituals. Young people are more likely to do things in their own way. We see boys and girls marking their maturity with increasing violence and vandalism. Gangs identify themselves by the style of tattoo or piercings they have, the clothing they wear, their patterns of speech and the actions they are required to undertake in order to 'belong'. Initiation takes many forms. In its most extreme variant, we now see initiation rites on the streets of big cities like London and Chicago involving knives and guns being used on innocent victims to prove strength and implacable loyalty to the group. Inevitably, drugs will play a role.

Tony: But that suggests this behaviour is specific to adolescents. The desire to express belonging through visual images or belonging to a group isn't just an adolescent phenomenon.

Herb: True: identifying with an admired celebrity or belonging to a glamorous lifestyle through a physical statement occurs in all age groups. With adolescence, though, the experience can be more intense. Witness the Beckham/Bieber fashion trends for pervasive body tattoos. Not so long ago tattoos were only for navvies and sailors, but for some teenagers, being able to sport one becomes a matter of the greatest significance. In any event, the fashion wheel will turn, and tattoo-removal will become a profitable plastic-surgery sideline.

Tony: It isn't so much the extremes of behaviour that strike me but that the impact of modernity on ancient rituals has meant there are few straightforward steps into adulthood. As a consequence, there is a dislocation between the generations as it becomes harder to identify with what has happened before. This leads to conflict. It also runs the risk that individuals in contemporary society never mix properly, never settle down and have no cultural identity or sense of real belonging. In any event, it's not obvious what they would belong to.

Herb: It wouldn't be accurate to say there are no formal, ritualistic rites of passage in contemporary society, but they tend to be religious. What is interesting is the dramatic decline of secular rites of passage. In boys the signs of growing up, such as the growth of facial hair and other physical manifestations of puberty, tend not to be celebrated, unlike the first sign of breast development and the onset of periods in girls. These have become personal matters rather than communal or cultural. It's a good example of how we have polarized into multiple groups with different ideas of validation and different ways of looking at the world. The West has always had at its heart the idea that the individual is special and uniquely formed.

Tony: As a teacher, I believe young people should be strongly encouraged to feel they can shape their own destinies, but only as part of a larger cultural picture. One of the besetting problems in the West is the glorification of ambition and the individual goal above all else. The unique, personal journey is fine as rhetoric, but I've seen the collateral damage on young people. I once met a highly articulate 12-year-old boy from a poor background who kept talking about his 'journey', and setting out the daunting career trajectory that would be his. It became apparent that he had nothing else to say on any other topic, and precious little detail as to how this journey would actually happen. He had been told that if you believe in your dream enough and say it often and loud enough, then somehow it will happen. The poor boy had been led by adults into a cul-de-sac. The real person was not being allowed to emerge. His final flourish was to produce a commercially produced autobiography entitled *My Journey*. I subsequently banned all use of the word 'journey' in discussions about pupils!

Herb: What you describe is part of a bigger issue. The drive for an excess of material possessions, or for a very particular body shape, creates a set of hyperbolic models impossible for anyone to grasp. It's a way of building in dissatisfaction with one's lot. In tribal communities girls will be taken away into initiation classes and taught the things their community perceives essential for them to know, much of it to do with domestic organization. They return to the group with a strong sense of identity and a good sense of belonging: feeling good about themselves as functioning adults in society. Much the same happens with boys, who learn the realistic expectations of their community. Both sexes leave their homes as children and return as adults. To a modern Western eye this process seems extraordinarily limiting: no one is expected to look beyond the horizon – but it offers clarity and comfort.

Tony: Received wisdom suggests there are three factors which greatly influence our psychological development: what goes on in our own heads, what goes on in our immediate surroundings, and what goes on in society as a whole. For young people in school, what they believe other people think is of great significance, frequently greater than either facts or evidence. Any sense of a direct route through rites of passage is lost in the curling mists of perception.

Herb: That's certainly true. A teenager will frequently have a binary view of themselves: for example, 'I see myself as ugly'; 'I think I'm shy'; 'I think I'm uninviting'; and so on – yet others, both adults and their peer group, may have a completely different perception, regarding that individual as attractive, outgoing and good company. This distortion is particularly true in relationships that can be described as 'bullying'. I've found it very common for teenagers to resort to simplistic descriptions of behaviour: 'Other people get at me all the time'; 'I'm defending myself'. Surviving bullying is often managed by associating with a powerful, if nasty, individual admired by everyone else. What is surprisingly common, and known as identification with the aggressor, is to join a group or attach to an individual in order to be perceived as one of the in-crowd, even to the extent of aiding an aggressor so that you're not a victim yourself.

Tony: This very basic human need to belong permeates all age groups, but often seems at its most intense and heartfelt among 12- to 15-year-olds, pretty much to the exclusion of everything else. It drives a great deal of behaviour in schools.

Herb: A 13-year-old boy came to see me in a terrible state. He couldn't stop himself shivering and crying. It transpired that three older boys in his boarding house had decided to use him as a plaything, to the extent that they were tearing up his work, messing up his room and hiding his possessions. The boy had settled into the school well until this victimization had begun. A few days later, a member of staff in the boarding house overheard the three planning what they saw as another prank to be played against the younger boy. I asked the deputy head to tell them it would be a good idea if they made their minds up as to whether they wished to stay at the school, and go home for the weekend to think about it. This is what happened. What was particularly interesting was the reaction of the parents. One in particular, who was very important in the legal world, could not deal with the cheek of a 'simple therapist' asking the school to exclude his son: another joined him in righteous indignation. The other parents, however, agreed this was exactly what the boys needed.

Tony: How did you deal with the aggressive legal man?

Herb: I wrote a long letter on my professional letterhead, explaining what I had done and why I had acted as I did. I'd be very happy, I added, to meet him. There was no response.

Tony: And what happened when the boys returned?

Herb: I held a group session with them where we discussed bullying and why it was bad for them to develop into the kind of individual who would perpetrate such distress and, indeed, be perceived as such by others. In the event, a year or so later one of them turned out to be the younger boy's best friend. That aggressor and victim should subsequently be able to form a strong bond is not that unusual, and should give hope to parents and young people. In other words, these bullying situations, that can seem so terrible at the time, are not the end of the world. They may not exactly be a rite of passage, but they are sidetracks that have to be negotiated while growing up. It was helpful in this instance that news of the event travelled round the school, so a lot of pupils realized that prolonged bullying would lead to action by the authorities. As a headmaster you must have seen lots of cases like this.

Tony: Yes, plenty. It always amazes me when one hears headteachers claim there's no bullying in their school. I wonder if they've ever truly looked at what's in front of them. There's bullying in some form in every community. The issue is how the community deals with it.

Herb: It seems to me the important thing is to be open about it and engage in constructive conversation.

Tony: As you discovered, spiky, even corrosive relationships can become positive and life-enhancing. It might sound odd to say it, but out of bullying can come real learning and stronger relationships, and there is at least an element of rite of passage about it.

You talk about getting antagonists together as a group. I've seen this happen on a number of occasions. Indeed, bringing together a group of teenagers who have been bullying one another, to sit and talk about the whole experience, has proved salutary. I remember one utterly dysfunctional group of 14-year-olds subsequently all becoming such strong friends that they went on holiday together. The shared experience of bullying and its aftermath, it seemed, actually brought them closer together. A key to eventual success was the school making it clear that the bullies' behaviour was unacceptable and that sanctions would be imposed, then insisting on structured meetings with an experienced adult. This wasn't a swift turn-around. Indeed, it took months. The psychology of this is fascinating.

Herb: It's a two-pronged thing. The first and more important element is simply, 'We're watching you, and what you're doing.' The second is enabling young people to empathize: to put themselves in the victim's shoes and feel the consequences of what they are doing to someone else.

Tony: We seem to be agreeing that the process of learning from one another is key to resolving some of the difficulties faced during adolescence. It strikes me, however, that many schools don't see it this way, but rather operate a 'zero-tolerance policy' which is a kind of shortcut.

It may make life easier for the school, but it's tantamount to a form of bullying in itself. It's too easy for a school to hide behind protocols and take the safe, legally approved course of action. On a number of occasions as a headmaster I was advised by lawyers that I should offer no pastoral support at all to a family whose child might be in serious trouble for a particular offence: the legal argument appeared to be that if he or she was bad enough to merit possible exclusion, then the school shouldn't muddy the waters. This seems to me fundamentally wrong. There are occasions when a school may be exposed, but in most cases genuine progress can be made simply by talking with the family. And it's worth the legal risk. Being removed from a school doesn't mean that there's no future. What's far more important is a young person's healthy long-term development, and this may necessitate a change of school. That individual learns and grows, which is a rite of passage.

Herb: That should be a cheering thought for parents! Good mental-health support and guidance should indeed be available to all involved.

Tony: I wonder if there's a danger that the word 'adolescence' has become an umbrella term for a variety of different phases. Generally speaking, adolescence is talked about in terms of its pre-, early, middle and late stages. These definitions need some teasing out, because they refer to different types of experience.

Herb: Adolescence and puberty are completely different phenomena, and must be recognized as such. Some girls nowadays start having their periods and develop breasts much earlier than their mothers and grandmothers – evidence suggests as a result of better nutrition and increased weight. To some extent this is happening with boys as well, with voices breaking and even some breast development occurring earlier.

In both sexes, irritability is the norm, not the exception, as it always used to be. To a great extent pre-adolescence and adolescence overlap. Middle adolescence, defined as the most crucial period of school, between the ages of 15 and 19, has become an increasingly arbitrary distinction: we now see adolescence running through to the late 20s. What's interesting is the difference between the increasing numbers of young people who, by going to college or university, stay with their peers, and those who go into apprenticeships or straight into work. There can be less support from agemates for the latter group, but they receive an enormous amount of training from mature adults with whom they then identify. It's a case of 'When in Rome, do as the Romans . . .'

Tony: There's a good argument that structured apprenticeships offer a more effective rite of passage than some flabby degree courses. Adolescence has traditionally been described as the four phases you've just itemized, but I wonder if this has any value today, when there seems to be so much overlap and so much acceleration of the process of adolescence, and traditional fixed points have shifted.

Herb: Yes, there is a continuing shift, not so much in individual experiences, but ever more powerfully in the impact of outside forces, particularly social media, on how young people function.

Tony: So we seem to be saying that adolescence gradually appears around the age of 9, and gradually blends into full adulthood in the late 20s.

Herb: That's probably right. Rather than vainly trying to set boundaries, it's easier to see it as starting with or around the time of puberty, and continuing right through to when people are more or less on the pathway they are likely to stay on for the rest of their lives.

Tony: Part of the difficulty in drawing lines must be the extent to which even quite young children mimic adult behaviour, whether in the real or virtual world. This mimicking must have an effect on their development.

Herb: I've seen my own seven- or eight-year-old grandchildren developing or mimicking adult characteristics – even a young girl, for example, can be fascinated by make-up, fashion and body shape, as a result of images powerfully promoted on television and through advertising and peer pressure. It's difficult for parents to try and stop your child copying what most other children in their class are doing: it's better, while they're adjusting to what is happening around them, to try and re-shape their experiences within your set of norms. I can't emphasize enough how rapidly all this is changing, and how frightening it is for adults.

Tony: Perhaps by stressing all this change and complexity we're in danger of painting too bleak a picture In essence, adolescence is a rite of passage because it's about moving on.

Herb: In one sense it's clear-cut. Adolescents are young people who are going to school, getting educated, absorbing family ideas, developing thoughts along religious and social lines and beginning to formulate a coherent sense of themselves as individuals. In the end, it's the process of breaking out from the family.

Tony: Yet 'family' can be defined in a number of ways. There are many types of family and pseudo-family – the groupings we create at school, for example.

Herb: In the past, the extended family has been a very important part of growing up, with aunts, uncles, older cousins and older siblings all having influence on how young people talk, walk and dress, and to some extent this extended family has mitigated the controlling influence of home and school. But the traditional extended family has increasingly become a victim of social mobility, dissipating and even undoing altogether for many young people a whole network of relationships and role models. So the focus has turned very much on the immediate family living at home, with the consequence, one can argue, that relationships at school have become much more significant.

Tony: Most teachers would recognize the truth of that. Educating the whole person has long been a mantra of the British school tradition, but the pressure on schools to solve a welter of social problems has grown significantly. You've acknowledged that there are still moments in the lives of young people today that can be said to offer some kind of rite of passage, but the main difference between the relative certainties of the past and contemporary society, it seems, is the lack of what might be called 'standardization', or at least some way of measuring what the norms are. We are not peas in a pod, but nowadays it seems there is no pod at all!

Herb: That's certainly true when it comes to money. Money plays a role in almost everything we do, and for many, social position depends on net worth and the appearance of wealth. How we establish that position in turn inevitably revolves around the extent to which we've changed, or gone through some rite or role change in our life. I could go on about fashion, the use of make-up, dieting, plastic surgery – a whole host of things deemed to change our role in and gain for that individual a better way of functioning. Here, perhaps, are our contemporary rites of passage. Consumption and celebrity are now firmly established as social lode stars, and aspired to by many young people who see such things around them most of the time.

The continuity, however, is that adolescence has always been about identity and progress into a coherent adult life.

Tony: So what can we say to parents about channelling that deep-rooted human impulse for rites of passage constructively and meaningfully for young people?

Herb: We need to recognize that the many important transitions which take place all our lives are in many respects not so different from many years ago: first girl- or boyfriend, coming-of-age parties, moving into a job, apprenticeships or further education, graduation. All are moments to be grasped and celebrated. Each stage should be well marked out for healthy mental development.

Tony: This is why the rituals of school life are so important, from the first day at school, wearing a uniform as a sign of belonging, the daily routine of assemblies and lessons, to speech days, team selection, year-group discos, even exams and, of course, leaving school. Without rituals a school would be like a busy railway concourse: all endless bustle and everyone head-down off in their own direction – no connection, no sense of community.

Herb: They lay a foundation. They mark stages of responsibility: from formal education to first job; permanent commitments such as marriage, children, grandchildren and even retirement. And then to death, which we should celebrate as warmly as every other stage.

Tony: This suggests a healthy adolescence prepares you for death.

Herb: Odd though it sounds, exactly so.

3

i. So What is Normal?

Tony: Throughout history, mankind has had a habit of categorizing experience into groups in order to make more sense of it. As a psychiatrist, you talk about the five elements to life.

Herb: I'm referring to a number of different headings to categorize our psychological development: family, friends, future, school and sex, in no particular order, as problems can arise in any of these, with many overlaps. Together they constitute the psychological self: they make us who we are. Inevitably, throughout all developmental stages, each impacts to a greater or lesser extent on the others. Unsurprisingly, physical elements of growth – height, weight, general appearance, distinctiveness and so on – are an essential part of the process of development. When we meet someone, we consciously or unconsciously make an instant judgement – first impressions really do count! This is entirely normal, but without discounting the importance of physical appearance, for the therapist or psychiatrist it's the inner self that is more crucial to evaluate.

FAMILY

Tony: Your first heading is family. Even with the most loving individuals, family life can be something of a battleground, but one essential for learning how to develop healthy relationships.

Herb: So much happens within family life. So many issues that might fall under other headings bubble to the surface here – issues such as poverty, physical illness, family hierarchy, parental problems, whether financial or emotional, adoption, acceptance of friends and so on. A key issue is eating. Eating habits are often a very good barometer of healthy development during adolescence: 'when', 'what', 'where' and 'if at all'.

Tony: But family life is far from the only influence on the developing child and adolescent.

Herb: From birth to the beginning of adolescence the building blocks of the future are being formed, but we can't assume this shaping is only happening within family, or indeed among friends or at school. There are many unexpected outside forces constantly bombarding the developing child, and therefore forming and re-forming the eventual outcome. These influences continue to change us throughout our lives: nothing is fixed and immutable.

Tony: It's sometimes said that all families are dysfunctional; that the paradigm of a healthy, happy family is just an illusion.

Herb: I doubt there is a family which has been entirely problem-free at all stages. As we used to say at medical school, it would be 'as rare as rocking-horse manure'! All families have difficulties, and we have to get over it and get on with it, always remembering that love and care, despite sometimes appalling situations, are the main healers. It's good to remind yourself that 'it will pass.'

Tony: Sadly, this applies to the good times as well, but that's all part of life. We need to be clear what we mean by the term 'family'. For many years the ideal of the 'nuclear family', typified by mother, father, 2.4 children and a stable extended family, has been rooted in the public imagination, but in our modern society there is such fragmentation and mobility that the extended family network, of cousins and even older siblings, for instance, may have little if any part to play in the way the life of a young person unfolds. This is a big difference from the relatively recent past. We also know that there are many different permutations of family – same-sex parents, for example – that can work well. In a society that is mutating and adapting at considerable speed, I wonder how much it really matters now whether a child has both a mother and a father figure.

Herb: That's a very good question for the 21st century. There's little doubt that the ordinary nuclear family is still seen as the norm, a kind of default position, but the ground under this norm has shifted significantly, and continues to do so. There are many children who do not live with both biological parents. I would happily concede that I have come across single parents, of both sexes, who have created very good homes, providing excellent formative bases for children to develop in a way which by any measure would be seen as loving and effective. Indeed, some of the most successful children I've met have been brought up by different types of parental figures – for example, mother and a girlfriend, or father and a boyfriend. These are not the kind of parents who inevitably need professional help.

We know that families constituted in different ways can function very well indeed.

Tony: As a teacher I had on many occasions to deal with a child in difficulty, and it was only when I met the child's parents that I began to understand exactly why there was a problem. The 15-year-old boorish bully, for example, with a father who was a bigger boorish bully. The flaws of the parents seemed to have been writ large in the child's experience. It's clear that role models are important in family life, but I've dealt with many families, and I'm struck by the parents who are first-rate role models yet face considerable difficulty with their child. There doesn't seem to be rhyme or reason. Who knows what it is that really makes families work well?

Herb: There's no simple answer. We tend to recognize problems when we see and feel them. 'Like father, like son' sounds neat enough, but it isn't always true. Subconscious reaction-formation is very interesting – 'I do/don't like what I am experiencing.' The young person will mimic adult behaviour, or reject it, and act accordingly. So it's possible, for example, for a child to react against what is seen as an unreachable, high parental role model.

The concept of rules and regulations should be flexible and open to adaptation, albeit with the understanding that there is an acceptance of the family's expectations. These might include normal keeping of hours, rules about assisting around the house, perhaps even the signing of a contract agreeing to accept family values and rules. Normality is a broad church, and very difficult to define. In the past, a normal family could be seen as one in which everyone does everything by the book, and in which nothing ever goes wrong. This is the stuff of fairytales.

Tony: In *Anna Karenina*, Tolstoy remarks that 'Happy families are all alike; every unhappy family is unhappy in its own way.' Is he right?

Herb: Tolstoy is writing about a different culture, place and time, and he polarizes just two types of family. It rolls off the tongue easily, but there is much more to it than that.

Tony: Well, that's Tolstoy dealt with! Let's turn to our own age. It's certainly true that unconventional families can lead a perfectly contented existence, and also true that neither happy nor unhappy families have a monopoly on particular outcomes for their children. There are many situations where critical, truculent and downright unpleasant teenagers have parents who are hugely well-intentioned and have done their very best. That said, there are also cases where parents have manifestly got things wrong, or at least not had the skills to shape a healthy relationship with their children. I've had parents in my study sobbing with frustration and embarrassment, unable to understand why their child did what he or she did.

Herb: It would be very fanciful indeed to suppose that the world our children now face is entirely like the one we faced at that age, let alone in Tolstoy's period. For example, it's a surprise to find recent research revealing that the incidence of smoking, drinking and teenage pregnancies in the Western world is actually falling, when not long ago it was believed to be rising to an unacceptable level. The reasons may be quite difficult to determine, but the influence of social media in almost every part of a young person's life cannot be over-estimated. Almost all opinions, ideas, functions, even education these days, come from or are at least shaped by the internet and social media.

Tony: The internet and social media have clearly had a seismic impact on our behaviour and relationships, but they have had an indirect effect on family life by influencing the way families connect. I hear of parents and children communicating by text even in the home, perhaps even at the same table. Sometimes a text is a way of avoiding eye contact, especially after an argument!

Herb: One of the most striking changes is the way we eat, whether together, individually, or in groups. It's often said that the family that eats together, lives and thrives together, but in the 21st century that's clearly not going to happen with all families.

Tony: Food is an issue that merits a chapter in its own right. I can see that how families deal with food is a bellwether for family relationships generally, but there are changing expectations around behaviour, about what's seen to be acceptable. Many old-fashioned courtesies, like giving up a seat on a bus to an older person for example, have largely disappeared. Indeed, it can be disconcerting for a teenager nowadays to find themselves actually chastised by an adult for having the temerity to offer a seat! Parents drawing on their own childhood experiences can seem and feel out-of-touch.

Herb: How sad that common courtesies can lead to hostile responses. But if outcomes are different from expectations, why take the chance? A prime example of how parents find themselves having to deal with their children in a very different way from the family life they knew as children, is that whereas defiance and destructive behaviour used to be rare, they seem to have increased greatly as social mobility and social media have affected children's self-awareness.

Tony: The notion of normality changes all the time. Our perceptions may shift almost imperceptibly, but looking back we see just how much has changed. There are now growing concerns about children's emotional and mental well-being. Governments have hitherto tended to focus on physical health rather than the mental side, yet mental health problems seem to be increasing at an alarming rate.

Herb: This is certainly what I have experienced. Mental-health expenditure has been regarded as the soft underbelly of healthcare programmes, and thus has been the worst financed. There is more pressure on modern families than ever before, and mental distress of one kind or another is a byproduct. In part this is a consequence of some traditional boundaries disappearing, so the old certainties are less clear. Family rules, for example, are often unenforceable for a number of reasons: the beatings that some of us received when we were disobedient are now, rightly, forbidden. Sanctions are almost impossible to impose, and almost always revolve around pocket money or expenditure on clothing, make-up, social life and so on.

Tony: Looking back, I realize I was part of the cusp generation: I was beaten as a young schoolboy, but by the time I started teaching in my early 20s never even contemplated hitting children. What stays in my mind is not the technical efficiency of the infamous 'Foster chop' (named after its creator, who used the metal edge of a ruler like a bacon-slicer on the stinging posterior of a ten-year-old as punishment for the sin of talking), but the professional inadequacy of the teacher: he had no other sanction in his repertoire. With the demise of corporal punishment, teachers have been obliged to become better teachers. The same is true of parents, challenging though that may be.

Herb: Another significant change has been sleep patterns. Much of this can be attributed to the dominance of the smart phone. Identification with parents is far less powerful than it used to be, not least in the context of sexual orientation. The differences which were hidden under the carpet have become more exposed, and by and large more understandable and acceptable.

Tony: Despite this litany of pressure and difficulty, is it not also the case that we are healthier, wealthier and possibly wiser than any generation that precedes us?

Herb: Broadly speaking, I think that's true, though we are not necessarily much happier.

FRIENDS

Tony: As a counterpoint to the stresses and strains of family pressure, friendship with peers can be a tonic. In school one of the heartening things is how individual and group relationships can develop –the unlikely bond between teenagers of completely different interests and temperament, for example. I remember as a teenager feeling the warmth and sheer pleasure of friendships that took the sting out of the difficult things. Teenage togetherness offers tremendous benefits, but the issue of friendship, just like relationships with parents, is a complex one. The dynamics of friendship can lead to troubled times for young people, as they form groups and seek out their own identity.

Herb: Important, too, is the extent to which self-image varies when seen through the prisms of different relationships. For example, parents might make you think you are the most wonderful, brilliant, beautiful, artistic creature on earth, whereas your friends' perception of you might be completely different. Friends can become a more honest and reliable secondary family and, as such, one to trust more.

Tony: In that case the natural instinct would be to disbelieve your parents on the grounds that they would say that, wouldn't they? Being told by a parent that she is the most beautiful and well-dressed will reinforce a younger child's confidence whenever she talks to her peers, but by the time she is a teenager she is more likely to discount the positive things her parents say about her and be inclined to believe negative comments from her peer group.

Herb: Absolutely, and thereon hang a number of problems. Parents need to understand that there are many types of family group. There are young people who for a variety of reasons have no friends, or far too many superficial contacts; there are those who gather in groups which may or may not be acceptable; there are those who join the kind of group with an almost street-gang quality, in which bullying and control of others predominates, and some will end up as victims and some as participants. None of these groupings are cast in stone. Young people can be constantly moving from one group to another. Parental acceptance of friends is another very big issue. More often than not it works both ways. Parents taking a dislike to one of their child's friends may act as a great dampener on the friendship – or have exactly the opposite effect. If a mother takes strong exception to a particular person with whom her child has a close relationship, then to some extent she is alienating that child. This has to be understood and managed very carefully.

Tony: The key thing in situations like this is for parents to be open, welcoming and alert, and keep a dialogue going. If you welcome your child's friends into the home, then you will learn a great deal about your own child from talking to them – other people's children are often more talkative than your own. You'll then be better placed to make reasonable judgments.

Herb: And if a child's friends refuse point-blank to come back home with them at all, that puts their parents in a strong position for a sensible conversation with them about relationships, and the problems of divided loyalties.

Tony: We have touched on gang-like behaviour. Group dynamics during the teenage years are a fascinating issue in themselves. Some years ago I was surprised to read in a survey of gangs in New York – groups of violent young men who appear to the outside world to be aggressive and abnormal – that the prime motivations for being part of the gang were identity within the group, respect from peers and, most interesting of all, experiencing love. Love is not a word we would normally associate with a violent gang, but there are very powerful reasons for wanting to belong somewhere. It's the kind of relationship that binds pupils together in a good boarding school. In that sense it's a short step from a New York gang to a place like Eton. It's interesting how little it can take to tip the needle on the dial one way or the other in a particular set of relationships: it leads in one group to positive outcomes, while another group seems set on driving itself over a cliff.

Herb: Our many instincts enable us to survive, and one of the most significant, in terms of day-to-day functioning, is the herd instinct. We have a desperate need to belong, and on occasion this can lead us to extremes. The importance to our individual psychology of being part of groups simply cannot be overestimated. In 1905 Gustav Le Bon wrote in *The Crowd* that a group is not simply the sum of all the individuals in it, but a new psychological entity in itself. When people are caught up in the heady intoxication of being with others they end up doing things they would never have dreamt possible. A kind of collective irresponsibility can develop, leading to behaviour that can be dangerous or even illegal or both.

Tony: We see this when people get caught up in a chanting crowd at a football match, or when something triggers the actions of a mob. We see it in school sometimes, too, when a kind of spirit of bacchanalia grips otherwise dutiful teenagers in a desire to cut the traces, make a lot of noise and generally be a pain. After the event, individual teenagers will genuinely find it hard to explain why they did what they did. They just don't know: the group had taken over.

Herb: It can happen in any social grouping and in any situation. I well remember one young man who was a great success socially with his peers, and academically too, but was also involved in extreme political groups. He was caught up in a major demonstration in a big city and ended up smashing windows, turning over cars and setting light to as many things as he could. He was easily identified as one of the perpetrators and ended up in court, where the judge gave him a stiff sentence as a deterrent to others. His parents, of course, were beside themselves.

Tony: In the case you cite, the need to belong seems overwhelming. It seems to be innate: humans are social animals. Despite the extreme cases, this desire to belong is also very positive and life-enhancing. It's wonderful seeing young people discovering the joy of community, if sometimes rather exuberantly and to the irritation of adults! Or the immature, timid boy screaming with boisterous delight when he's eventually accepted into a game by his peer group. As a teacher, I was far more concerned about those young people who found it hard to read social connections and know how to belong, than those who were loud and occasionally lacked restraint.

Herb: It's perhaps a stereotype, but true nevertheless, that completely isolated individuals who have no sense of friendship with anyone are among the most disturbed people in society, and consequently the ones most likely to do the most terrible things. We see it all too frequently with mass shootings in schools, for example. Such extreme cases involve people who may be psychotic and require medical interventions including hospitalization and medication. In a more normal context, young people who feel themselves to be outside the herd can suffer many torments, so powerful is that urge to belong. Unfortunately this situation is not uncommon. Large numbers of young people fall into the autistic spectrum group (ASD) and/or attention deficit hyperactivity disorder (ADHD). They can often be distressed and unhappy or isolated, and easy meat for the bully.

Tony: In adult life, we have a great deal of choice about which groups or herds we end up belonging to. When we are young and our sense of self is still insecure, it's a tougher proposition. Furthermore, when you are in school your choice of whom you associate with on a daily basis is rather limited. It's difficult to predict the chemistry of a group, to the dismay of those parents who think schools should be able to create harmonious bubbles. An increasing minority of parents seek to create a perfect, bespoke world for their child by actually demanding they be placed in a particular class or house. Schools simply cannot provide this, nor should they, but good schools will still know how to develop the culture of groups. I'm afraid this happens less frequently than it should, however: I've spent a lifetime in schools, and have to acknowledge that they can be crucibles of despair as well as places of hope and bright futures.

Herb: Fortunately, the majority of young people do well in school socially and academically, often because they have wide-ranging interactions. A limited choice of relationships can lead to feelings of insecurity and prompt the individual to turn to gangs. Belonging to one offers a sense of safety, as you've noted – rather like finding an accepting family. When a supportive family dynamic is weak or absent altogether this can seem particularly attractive.

Tony: It's often said that the key factor is the lack of an effective male role model for young men as they grow up, but it strikes me that's not always the case: as we've observed, there are many examples of single parents successfully raising children.

Herb: Add to all this the powerful cultural and sub-cultural groupings in every society. A single mother with four children all by different fathers who have no apparent interest in their offspring is faced with an extreme manifestation of family life which may lead to behavioural and developmental problems among those children – or may not. We know generalizations may be nice to look at, but don't necessarily apply to individuals. Every human being has to be viewed in his or her own right.

Tony: Another example of generalization is that we tend to speak of gangs as comprising potentially violent young men, but nowadays girl gangs are becoming more active, which can be far more aggressive and frightening than a group of boys.

Herb: This is the negative side of a positive development. Over recent years gender roles have become less rooted in traditional expectations. Girls are encouraged to do what boys are doing, even outdoing them in some respects.

Tony: That doesn't mean girls should outdo boys in negativity.

Herb: True, but I think girls are saying to themselves, whether consciously or unconsciously, 'I can do anything the boys can do.' What interests me is that while teenagers tend to feel more comfortable in same-sex groups, when mixed-sex gangs develop there tends to be a greater degree of aggression and confrontation.

FUTURE

Tony: The third of your headings intrigues me, because in a way it's the least tangible. You talk about the future having a lasting and profound influence on the way young people will grow up.

Herb: We've touched on the different stages of adolescence. We tend to see younger adolescents as being easier to deal with at home and less concerned about the enormity of what lies ahead, but a feature of today's generation is how even quite young adolescents are exercised about the future.

Tony: For many years we've understood that adolescence is a crucial period for coming to terms with personal identity and one's place in the world, and it seems this process is now happening earlier. There are plenty of examples: a primary school child expressing concern about international relationships in the Brexit era; a 13-year-old crippled by anxiety about global warming. There's a welter of news and views bombarding the young, and it takes a degree of sophistication to make sense of it. A young generation is developing digital skills their parents never had, but I'm concerned that they struggle to deal with all this information: it's tough enough for adults.

Herb: Partly they are not equipped because so much of what is happening to them is not within their parents' own experience. But what concerns me particularly is the level of anxiety I now see at the pre-teen stage. Young people have access to information of which their parents and teachers have little knowledge, from sexual expectations to fringe politics, and they haven't developed the filtering mechanisms which enable them to make sense of what they see and hear.

Tony: Likewise, I've noticed how some young people are worried that in a fragmented world the relative certainty of a linear future seems to have been taken away from them. There are not the clearly defined pathways there once were. When I was 18, it was assumed I should become qualified in some area and follow it through for a lifetime career: train as a lawyer, become a judge. No longer. This lack of direction for the future can seem daunting, yet there are also many teenagers who feel liberated and excited about the life ahead.

Herb: That may be because you've been lucky enough to have worked in successful schools.

Tony: I accept that, and I'm well aware that there are significant numbers of teenagers who appear to have no worries of any kind about a career – or, indeed, any interest in their planet – but that has probably always been the case. We need to encourage all school pupils to be engaged in everything around them.

Herb: While at the same time creating that crucial filtering mechanism. The fake news phenomenon has taken off with a vengeance.

Tony: Certainly the ability to distinguish between fake and sound information is, or should be, central to a good education. Young people have to deal with more treacherous shifting sands than their parents ever did, largely because of the sheer volume and availability of unverified information through social media. Related to that is the ability to arrive at critical judgements based on evidence which take into account circumstance and context. It's a tall order: we would like the generations that follow us to have deep and unwavering values that will see them through life, but they also need the ability to change perspective and see things from a variety of angles – that's how they will cope with what seems constant change. They need to be able to hold fast to what they perceive to be good and true, and yet at the same time be adaptable. This is a challenge for them, and inevitably has implications for their parents and for their schools.

Herb: And for the workplace and the way society operates.

Tony: A combination of adaptability and lasting values is difficult to achieve, but I'm not pessimistic. Uncertainty may cause worry, but it can also liberate imagination. I've seen teenagers come up with powerful, good ideas on a very large canvas, apparently unshackled by limitation – for example, setting out how to tackle huge global problems like hunger and poverty with a belief that they can make a difference. Youthful hope is part of the human condition, but I think it's more than that. Young people have the capacity to achieve remarkable things.

Herb: So what advice do you give parents about how they can help fuel this imaginative energy and positive thinking?

Tony: Talk and encourage! Talking to teenagers has often been seen as problematic, and there are certainly times, particularly in the middle-adolescent years, when parents need to learn how and when to do it, but there's a lot to be said for being gently persistent and creating a family expectation of talking about a whole range of topics. Mealtimes still provide a good opportunity, though shared family meals are increasingly rare. Take any opportunity. Analysing a football match can lead to a discussion about the morality of the money involved at the top of the professional game. One of the best opportunities is while driving, particularly when there is one parent and one teenager, both in front seats, both looking ahead. A closed space, a shared direction of travel and no eye contact can help create an atmosphere in which all kinds of things can be discussed.

Herb: An excellent example of pseudo-entrapment! Subjects normally taboo or impossible to bring up elsewhere can be tackled, helping both parties to move on.

SCHOOL (AND BEYOND)

Tony: Much about school life has remained comfortingly familiar over recent decades. Inevitably there are some challenging changes, the influence of the internet for example, but dealing with teenagers has had familiar rhythms over the years. What is more striking is the way some parental attitudes have shifted. Parents have always been ambitious for their children to achieve the very best, and that is a natural and positive thing. What I have seen is the rise of highly focused, targeted ambition in some parents, from London to Shanghai, fuelled by an obsession with measurable academic performance as a ticket to the next step. In what seems an ever more competitive, globalized world I can understand parents feeling anxious, but this attitude comes at a cost. It leads to great pressure and stress for young people. In parts of London it's reached an almost comic absurdity. Some parents can become obsessive about getting their child into the school of their choice at the age of two or three. It's as though in some strange, magical way this crucial decision will directly influence the child's chance of entry into Oxbridge. It's become a feeding frenzy. Schools themselves are partly to blame, but it's a bigger issue than that. The swelling desire of some parents vicariously to live their own ambitions through their children has been the cause of very significant damage to some young people.

Herb: I don't imagine it's just academic performance that excites parents.

Tony: It's the main source of angst, but all areas of a child's school life can be under intense scrutiny, which can lead to some worrying adult behaviour. For example, the father of a boy in a visiting football team repeatedly screaming in highly colourful language from the touchline that the (fully qualified) home-side referee is a cheat. In that case, I was delighted that the teacher/referee made a public show of abandoning the match. I've known parents who have demanded a particular part in a play for their child, and a fair number who have been highly selective about school rules. It's a kind of parental excess of zeal.

Herb: At the other end of the scale, there are too many parents or carers who show very little interest in their charges' everyday lives, including school. Somewhere in between I have come across those who simply want their children to go to school so they can get on with their own lives. That's very different from my own experience. The very concept of non-attendance or bad behaviour was unthinkable. When I was 14 I was caned by a teacher for bad behaviour and, rather unfortunately, when I went home I told my parents about it. I was punished yet again. There was certainly no sense of my parents rushing to the defence of their child, no matter what I had or hadn't done. The teacher was an authority figure: respect was due, and that was that.

Tony: This is part of a loss of faith in professions and in professional judgement generally. We have drifted into a belief that every individual somehow owns the right to be right.

Herb: One thing that strikes me, particularly in light of what you have just described about the football match, is the extent to which some teachers, certainly in the public sector, feel unsupported not only by parents but also by the system. This seems one of the reasons behind the great drop in the number of young people applying to become a teacher, which in the past was seen as a respected profession.

Tony: We should always beware the myth of the golden age. It's hard to find a time in our national history when teachers have really been celebrated, but it saddens me that having a good teacher is now equated less with a passport to a better life. Perhaps the image of the teacher as the route out of the mining village always was a little romantic, though there are plenty of successful people who will attest to the central role at least one teacher played in their lives. There's a contradiction in our contemporary view of teaching as a profession. In surveys of professions seen to have social value it still shows up very well, but in the next breath the same respondents place teaching towards the bottom of the scale of desired professions for their own children. Over the years I've noticed the relationship between teachers and parents becoming more transactional, as the belief has taken hold that schools are there to offer a service to a customer, and parents therefore have a right to a specific outcome on behalf of their child, sometimes whether the child wishes it or not.

Herb: This sounds as though it could be a feature of fee-paying schools.

Tony: You might think so, but in fact such aggressive behaviour is found in all types of school, and parents from all backgrounds can be pretty sharp-elbowed. I haven't had a knife drawn on me by a parent wishing to emphasize a point, as a headteacher friend of mine has, but I have been threatened with litigation in a heavy-handed way on a number of occasions. Friends and colleagues who are heads of different types of schools quote myopic parental reactions to all kinds of situations. Most parents, most of the time, are supportive and fair, but it's an ever more challenging environment for teachers and schools.

SEX

Herb: This is a vast area of discussion, especially with attitudes and interpretations changing so profoundly. Sexuality is almost always inevitably a confusional stage of development, but that confusion is much increased nowadays by a surfeit of information of all sorts and from all sides, some of it contradictory. Given the scale of the subject, it's better discussed in a chapter of its own.

SELF

Tony: All of the above leads us to the idea of the Self. Our self-image is crucial at any age, but it's intensely felt in the testing-ground of adolescence.

Herb: We were all young once, and often like to think we still are. Adolescents tend to focus on body shape, sporting and physical appearance, and whether or not they look good or unpleasant. *Am I attractive to other people?* Adolescents are particularly sensitive to the observations of others, but these tend to be in a coded form, so compliments are not necessarily believed, while criticisms are taken to heart. This is a natural enough reaction in all phases of our lives, but it's more acute in adolescence. Do we fit the pattern of our desired group?

Tony: This adolescent questioning can seem endless. *Am I in the place I want to be, physically/socially/ academically? Do I fit in with the group I want to be part of? Why am I not happy in my own skin?* It can sometimes sound like self-indulgence, but it's a necessary part of the search for identity.

Herb: It was Erikson who first discussed the subject of identity. His book *Identity, Youth and Crisis* has been a bestseller since its publication in 1968. He emphasized the complexity of identity in so-called advanced societies and the significance of role confusion. His work is important in developmental psychology, especially his description of the eight stages of psycho-social crises, largely in adolescence. This was in marked contrast to the work of Margaret Mead in Samoa and Malinowski with the Trobriand Islanders who focused on simple cultures in which there were only two gender roles, and therefore very few problems emerging in self-perception. This is a simplistic view, because sexual identity confusion must inevitably have occurred and been repressed. Humans have rapidly evolved socially into a complex culture. Role models such as mother and father can be outmoded and replaced by celebrities, teachers, sports people – there's a great number to choose from.

Tony: Geography plays a part, too. With increased social mobility, we are much less rooted to particular places than we once were, and influenced more by the culture of the environment our family has moved to – country, town, even suburb.

Herb: With greater freedom of movement, choice and individuality, there's more pressure on everyone to upgrade themselves in whatever way possible. Pressure comes, too, in having to decode blurred boundaries, with male and female roles now overlapping in most activities, except obviously pregnancy and birth. But even that has changed. It seems almost impossible to believe, but men who were assigned female sex at birth and have undergone a later trans procedure, may still have retained their original uterus. This has been used successfully to deliver, by Caesarean section, a fully developed baby from an implanted and fertilized egg.

Tony: The lines are blurred between the generations, too. Old and young are more likely to engage in similar activities or fashions, though the desire of teenagers to have their own territory still runs deep and adult invaders are not looked at kindly.

Herb: Add in the bombardment of information, much of it negative, from internet and social media, and it can be no surprise that many adolescents have a sense of the fragility of their identity.

Tony: A sensitivity to different identities is a good thing, but if it turns into a kind of relativism – anything goes, nothing is stable – then it will have a profound and demoralizing effect on the young.

In one sense identity is fluid, things change, but at any one time we need to feel confident about who we are. This can be bewildering for adolescents, and equally so and sometimes frustrating for their parents.

When faced by what appears to be disconcerting change, it can be helpful for parents to remember the constants:

1 Talk. Easy to say, sometimes difficult to do. Open channels for communication about little things can make a great deal of difference when there are troubles. You may need to be inventive about engineering situations where talking seems natural. And remember, what may not seem a problem to you, may loom large in a teenager's mind. So,

2 Listen. *Really* listen to what they are saying, not what you think they should be saying. It takes patience. There is no short cut.

3 Accept at all stages that your adolescent is a separate entity and not a carbon copy of parental ideas and views (or anyone else's). Developing personality is a complex thing, shifting and changing in response to different relationships and never fully fixed.

4 Criticize your adolescent's behaviour when your feel it is warranted – don't back off. But criticize their behaviour, not them. It's one thing to say, 'You are behaving badly and your behaviour is not acceptable,' another altogether to say, 'You're horrible.' Adolescents seem particularly sensitive to the distinction, and can infer rejection. All humans need to feel loved, especially adolescents. 'I will always love you, though I may not always like what you do.'

ii: The Normal Functions of the Brain

Without launching into a major science lesson, there are certain things about the brain's anatomy (what it looks like) and physiology (what it does) that everyone needs to know. A brain of sorts is the control centre for all living things: ants, worms, right up to human beings, with everything else in between. The most advanced brain development is in vertebrates, including fish and birds, but the greatest evolution has taken place in mammals: dogs, cats and everything from elephants to humans. Brain size is no indicator of efficiency and capabilities. The brain of a Chihuahua is very much smaller than that of a Great Dane, but the efficacy is identical. Weight for weight, humans have the largest brains of any mammal, and they're about the same size in all of us.

The way in which brains operate, that is to say their structure, is the same in all living things: the brain and the attached spinal cord are the command centre, the central nervous system (CNS). Its transmission service is the spinal chord and the attached nerves. The brain controls and interprets all our senses, such as smell, taste, sight, balance. The vast automatic nervous system (ANS) is the deputy, in charge of such things as digestion, heart function, breathing – all the things we don't usually think about but that are in constant operation in response to multiple stimuli. Most important in our general

THE HUMAN BRAIN

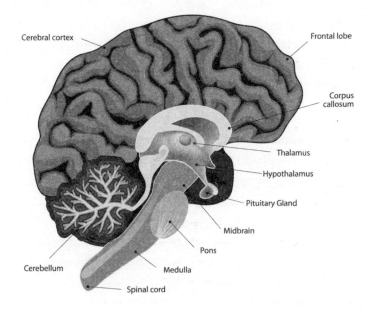

Cerebral cortex

Frontal lobe

Corpus callosum

Thalamus

Hypothalamus

Pituitary Gland

Midbrain

Pons

Cerebellum

Medulla

Spinal cord

functioning and development is the hypothalamus, which controls not only drinking and eating but also sleep and other cycles. It also controls the release of hormones from the pituitary gland, which is a pea-sized structure just below it. There are also many other crucial structures involved with our functioning, not directly relevant to us now. A helpful website is brainmadesimple.com.

Everything we think and do and act upon is overwhelmingly influenced by the great evolution of the forebrain (basically the cerebral cortex) in human beings. This is what makes us human, in contrast to the more primitive, instinctive behaviour of other mammals. Nevertheless, in all vertebrates a simple, painful stimulus to an extremity, like a pinprick on the finger, will elicit the same response.

A message is instantly sent to the brain via the spinal cord with a rapid return instruction to the muscles to contract and withdraw. The difference with humans is that we think about it.

One important area of the brain is the basal ganglia, which has a role in selecting our actions: rewards and punishments have the greatest effect in this area of the brain. Importantly, almost all that happens of no immediate consequence goes unnoticed by our unconscious mind, but is stored here. Difficulties in our emotional past fall somewhat loosely into this section of the brain: this is what some therapists attempt to explore when dealing with mental health problems.

HORMONES

Hormones occur in humans, but also in plants and most of the animal kingdom, and are best seen as chemical messengers from our glands, reaching most organs in the body in order to influence their functioning – sleep, sex, blood sugar, etc. They are part of an extremely intricate series of communications reciprocally affected by factors such as emotion, temperature and light.

Some hormones affect the release of others, and are almost always transported by the bloodstream. For example, Thyroid Stimulating Hormone (TSH) from the pituitary gland travels to the thyroid glands, affecting many parts of our animal functioning including growth and fat deposition. In adolescence in particular, sleep, hunger and mood variations are important functions of hormones: they lead to the onset of puberty and to stress, which in turn releases its own hormone, cortisol, from the adrenal glands. If this is complicated for adults to understand, what chance a teenager in the midst of it?

In addition to everything else, adolescents are assailed (if that is the word) by testosterone (in males) and oestrogen (in females). Testosterone derives from the testes in males and oestrogen from the ovaries in females, with the pituitary in the brain to some extent controlling what happens. The adrenal gland is also a significant producer of these hormones. All interactions are complex, not least because both males and females, particularly at puberty, have the hormones of the opposite sex affecting them one way or another. Some girls, for example, have wispy facial hair, and some boys may have breast enlargement. These phenomena are temporary, but often reassurance is needed.

Hormones play a major role in puberty. Although the hormones appear to be flying about wildly, it can be reassuring to know that there is a feedback system from the hippocampus to the pituitary in the brain which stops production when appropriate levels of them are present in the bloodstream.

Before looking at puberty, a word about the so-called *happy hormones*, the chemicals our bodies produce which are responsible for feelings of joy or pleasure or satisfaction, and which begin to exert their major influence during puberty. Conveniently, they form the acronym DOSE: dopamine, oxytocin, serotonin and endorphins. They are described in more detail in Chapter 8, Addictions.

PUBERTY

Puberty is a period of physical change which can be a dramatic and occasionally traumatic experience. It is affected by a range of factors, including genetics, culture, class, physical environment and diet. It also requires a psychological adjustment within families.

It starts in boys with testicular growth and the production of sperm. In girls, periods; pubic hair grows rapidly, with voice changes evident from the age of ten onwards in both sexes. Better diets and environment have led, in the Western world at any rate, to puberty starting at an earlier stage than used to be the case. Once it sets off, rapid growth is the most obvious feature. Girls are frequently bigger and stronger than boys of the same age, most likely for the only time in their lives.

Both sexes seem inordinately preoccupied with their bodies and the way they function and look. Girls usually go through a puppy-fat phase between the ages of 10 and 15 which can have serious implications for their self-image. Boys gain weight rapidly as well, continuing to do so until the age of 20 or so. For many boys one of the greatest embarrassments comes from their sudden high-pitched squeaking as their larynx changes shape (the loss of much-valued boy trebles) virtually overnight.

In the latter teenage years, body shape stabilizes: girls tend to slim down naturally and boys come to look increasingly masculine. There is a marked hormonal effect on the glandular activity of both sexes, producing oils on the skin and hair. This can lead to under-arm odour, which is easy enough to deal with, but also acne, which in some cases can become disfiguring and deeply embarrassing. Even in a milder form acne can last for many years, causing stress and creating an inhibiting, negative self-image that can permanently shape adult personality. Given the psychological effect it can have, it is perhaps surprising that it is sometimes not treated more seriously by doctors and families.

On the whole, it would seem that although girls are very shy about physical changes, boys appear to hate the experience much more, with greater unhappiness and embarrassment for reasons that are not entirely clear, but could derive from a need to demonstrate masculinity at a time when they are not fully in control of their bodies. Many boys develop breast enlargement (gynecomastia) which is usually short-lived, but can be extremely embarrassing: in both sexes breast growth is often asymmetrical, another source of discomfiture. Boys and girls can both become obsessive and self-regarding: concerns about bodies and appearance can be dominant and sometimes overwhelming at home and at school.

Rapid growth leads to clumsiness, as arms and legs grow longer and stronger but do not yet respond effectively to signals from the brain. Household items can be unintentionally sent flying, and it can seem as though there's a hooligan let loose in the house. Rapid growth can be painful, too, especially when it is uneven: an example is Osgood-Schlatter's disease, with pain in the knees when the bones in the legs grow at different rates. This is quite common in teenage boys – what is sometimes rather dismissively referred to as 'growing pains'. The best treatment is to lay off physical activity, like football, for a time, which for some boys can seem like purgatory.

Ironically, the advent of the smartphone has led to many teenagers spending part of the night awake with games or social media. This, in turn, causes problems with lack of sleep and focus during the day.

Genital growth in boys leads to increased sexual excitement and a sensitivity which can feel beyond control. Masturbation offers some relief. Meanwhile, girls have to deal with the onset of periods.

To cope with all of this, there is an apparent emotional withdrawal: that is to say, 'not hearing' what authority figures are saying. This is natural. Young people need to be alone some of the time: privacy becomes very important. As far as it is possible to do so, they need to have room within the home to retreat comfortably.

All this is part of the start of the struggle for independence from one's parents. What is a little surprising is that those adults who nag and seem to care are resented just as much as those who do not. For parents it can be a rough ride: they need to keep their eyes on the prize of grounded, responsive, grateful, lovely adult children. Parents need to play the long game.

SLEEP AND DREAMS

The ability to sleep well is one of our greatest gifts, and a human necessity. The adolescent mind and body require more sleep than adults; that is a biological fact. But it is also a family reality that arguments about bedtime/getting up/night-time distractions (such as smartphones) are part of the rhythm of life. It can be difficult for a teenager to accept that 17-year olds still need 9 hours sleep each night, and 13- year-olds up to 11 hours, especially if in their eyes that means going to bed too 'early'. In fact, there is good evidence to suggest that teenagers should sleep until about 9 a.m. and that the school day should start at 10 a.m. or later to fit their biorhythms, but a switch of that magnitude would precipitate a radical transformation in the lives of everyone in the workplace and the family which, at present, is hard to imagine. Trials in some schools are now taking place. Parents are left with a problem that stretches across the generations: how to educate their children into the habits of good sleep.

We talk about some of the difficulties in Chapter 9, Screenagers, but, in addition to the practical challenges, we need to have some understanding of the significance of dreaming.

Dreams have been the subject of debate since time immemorial. From the psychological angle, REM – that is, the Rapid Eye Movement part of sleep – is essential in brain developmental terms during infancy, which is why young children sleep so much more than adolescents and adults. It's easy to see the twitching and apparent active dreaming in small babies. It's believed that REM sleep stimulates those cerebral areas in which learning of all kinds is crucial. This is why some parts of the brain can be more active during the night than other sections, or than during the day, for that matter.

Freud felt that dreams are the pathway to the unconscious mind and, as such, crucially significant to what makes us who we are. Thinking is more active during these periods than would be the case when awake, because of the lack of distraction. At the other end of the argument, there are those who believe that so-called dreams are actually meaningless, and only made up of ideas experienced just before or just after full consciousness is reached. Many people still follow Freud's belief that exploring dreams in therapeutic situations leads to positive feelings, even when just discussed with friends.

Research relating to PTSD (Post Traumatic Stress Disorder), to nightmares and to the effects of noradrenaline, the stress hormone, suggests that when this hormone is at its minimum, that is to say in a state of relaxation, feelings of well-being and of peace in general are increased. This is when the effects of PTSD and its aftermath of emotional experiences are digested and appropriately dealt with.

As far as memory is concerned, it is believed that REM sleep is therapeutic. It co-ordinates and realigns all the happenings of the day in a comforting and healthy way. Conflict resolution, when the issues of the day are sorted out and made sense of, original thinking and problem-solving all happen during this stage of sleep, as does the ability to focus more effectively on study. It is the only period of the 24-hour cycle during which the brain is not influenced by anxiety-inducing noradrenaline. Non-REM sleep has its functions too, one of which is embedding memories more powerfully.

Sleeping and dreaming are not the same things: many individuals daydream, and have some of their best ideas during these semi-somnolent episodes, but regular, refreshing sleep at night is essential.

Everyone dreams, even if we don't recall our dreams subsequently. In truth, no one has yet definitively been able to identify why we dream, and why it seems so necessary to our day-to-day functioning and mental well-being. The important thing is to feel rested at the point of awakening when sound sleep has ended.

There are some real gifts we can give our children – the ability to read at an early age, for example, or consistent and stable relationships – but to reach these greater goals we need to inculcate in them a healthy attitude to diet and, especially, to sleep.

FIVE KEY THINGS YOU REALLY NEED TO KNOW ABOUT ADOLESCENTS AND THEIR BRAINS

1 *The adolescent brain is not joined up.* More particularly, the connections between the frontal cortex regions (the centre for higher-order integration of information needed for planning, strategizing, and goal-setting) have very immature links with the structures below, which stimulate appetite and risky behaviour and are poorly connected to the memory.

2 *Adolescents appear to see things in black and white terms.* Not surprisingly, motor and sensory functions develop a lot more quickly than the ability to make decisions and take control. Nine-year-olds soak up sensory experience in an undirected way. From puberty, children are driven to direct this sensory experience in order to gain a sharp response, whether vocal or physical – sometimes involving shouting or even hitting. Whether the feedback is positive or negative is less important than just getting a reaction. Adolescents will push and push for a reaction, often giving the impression of wanting a response in very black-and-white, either-or terms.

3 *Adolescents feed on risky behaviour.* Scientifically speaking, immature control systems (see above) can't channel the appetite for stimulation and reward, but there is more to it than that. There is an evolutionary impulse for an individual to leave a familiar and safe environment and take risks, in order to shape identity as an adult. Risky behaviour is an important part of growing up.

4 *Adolescents' perceptions are distorted.* Without the unburdened frontal lobes that filter our experience as adults, the stresses of life, such as social and family problems or illness, can (apparently disproportionately) lead to rude or bad behaviour.

5 *Everything goes out of the window when peers are involved.* Adolescents are particularly sensitive to the presence and influence of peer groups; they are stimulated by the attention of observers. Greater activity in the frontal cortex and striatum upgrades the potential value of the reward for risky behaviour, such as taking alcohol or drugs in order to appear a 'hero': the risk always seems worth it.

Some parents and teenagers will wonder what all the fuss is about, because their family experience has been of a seamless transition into adulthood. This does happen, as does every other permutation between seamless and traumatic. There is no template. The adolescent brain is bespoke to the individual.

These five facts explain a great deal about teenage behaviour, but they are all part of a normal, healthy and necessary process. And we should also remember that adolescence is one of the most creative periods in human life. The brain sparks a creativity that can be expressed in a myriad of ways, some of them unconventional, and all to be encouraged.

4

Parenting and Family Life

Tony: There are few jobs more worrying, contentious, universal and difficult than being a parent. Mother Nature made it pretty easy in most cases to become one, whether planned or unplanned, but how parenting is followed through, if at all, is a big subject.

Herb: This is especially the case for mothers. From the moment the pregnancy is confirmed and a decision taken to continue with it, there are so many anxieties, rules (what and what not to do), uncertainties and stressors that sometimes it's a wonder that most people do follow through. The must do's, such as keeping fit, diet, attending the right clinic and so on, are sometimes less difficult than the must nots, like avoiding alcohol and drugs, over-exercising and over-dieting, thus denying the foetus its essential nutritional ingredients for proper development. Fortunately, Mother Nature rides to the rescue once again, and almost everything that's required comes naturally, providing there is sufficient support, especially from the prospective father. Many women don't have that, but they can still be excellent providers, producing wonderful children, particularly with the help of an extended family and friends. There are no hard and fast rules for being a parent.

Tony: That's a crucial point. We have been ill-served over many years by notions of the perfect family. This is captured rather brilliantly at the end of the first episode of the TV show *Madmen*, when the slick, man-about-town advertising executive eventually returns home to his wife and two children (one boy and one girl, of course) to be caught in a freeze-frame as the ideal family – the very stuff of advertising in the 1960s. Sitcoms in particular can often be a reflection of social attitudes. For years perfect families (two parents and two children) were represented as good-looking and harmonious, with the odd setback but always happy endings. It's a vision that has never matched reality, yet sometimes there's still a yearning for this impossible ideal.

Herb: If we take it at its most basic level, parents are biological caregivers for their own children within their own species. We used to consider this solely in the context of male and female, but the changes in our society have been profound, with many variants, such as same-sex parents, all widely and quite properly accepted.

Tony: The best parents seem to be to be those who are happy within themselves and their lifestyles, and able to transmit this positive approach to their children, who then grow up secure and feeling nurtured and loved. But even then, parents who want their children to become independent-minded, healthy adults themselves in due course will face challenges and a bumpy ride.

Herb: The impression presented to the world might be misleading. For example, enforced conformity, with little interaction outside the family, might still be described by the individuals involved as 'being happy', but hides extraordinary vulnerability when the protective walls are taken down. Dysfunctional families might actually be those who seem totally contented with kindness and loving behaviour within their group. The reality might be a fallacious belief in their superior integrity, intellectual abilities and lifestyle, which can lead to extreme disillusionment when children eventually leave home. An inward-looking and self-regarding lifestyle is no preparation for what goes on everywhere else.

Tony: Your point about conformity is well taken. We are all different, and it's helpful for parents to have some understanding of how personality is formed. It is, after all, quite usual to know children of very different characters who share the same parents.

PERSONALITY

Herb: Essentially, our personality is how we present ourselves to the world at large. It includes aspects like calmness, compassion, confidence, charisma and sense of morality.

Tony: This seems a particularly fluid area. When it comes to personality types, definitions have come and gone, all the way back to Hippocrates.

Herb: Hippocrates named 4 types, Cattell 16 and Allport 4,000!

Tony: Quite. So what definitions, if any, do you think are relevant and helpful?

Herb: A Five-Factor Theory was developed in Cambridge some years ago which usefully identifies five personality types: openness, conscientiousness, extraversion, agree-ableness and neuroticism. For completeness' sake I might add introversion.

Tony: That's fine as far as professional categorization goes, but what matters to parents is how key aspects of personality evolve, and how much they can influence the process. As a very rough rule of thumb, I have taken it that about half of personality is dependent on genetics and about half is acquired.

Herb: That's indeed very rough, but it does make the point that genetics is not the overriding factor. It does seem the case, however, that genetics loads the gun and environment pulls the trigger. With sufficient conviction and determination we can change the way we function. This is easy to say, but how to put it into practice? The aspects people most want to exhibit in themselves are things like staying calm under pressure, always attempting to see the positive side of life, combatting withdrawal urges and being sociable and outgoing instead. An Australian study highlights traits we should be able to modify, and help our children to modify too. These include: enthusiasm and assertiveness as part of extraversion, politeness, compassion and empathy (and therefore agreeableness), positive thinking, being open-minded, imaginative and creative, being self-disciplined (with an orderly life based on routines), controlling mood volatility and so on.

Tony: So the first step would be to have a fuller awareness of your child's traits, identifying where you think there may be shortfalls. In the spirit of honesty, parents need to be self-critical about the kind of role models they themselves offer. It's common enough for desirable qualities to be more honoured in the breach. Parents need to bear in mind, too, that all family members influence one another. Compassion can be best learned between siblings, for example.

Herb: When attempting to understand young people, the best route is to have conversations aplenty, working through the situation in a methodical way to aid the appreciation of causes and consequences. Talk and more talk. It's through this kind of low-key, sensible and loving talking that young people come to develop the self-analytical skills they can apply to other situations.

Tony: A word I frequently hear from concerned parents about teenagers is 'attitude'. Attitude is not a fixed personality characteristic, and can change many times through a lifetime. Genetics plays a relatively small part. It's influenced by many different people, real and virtual, as well as the family. The advice you give above applies in the same way: talk it through. If the trenches are firmly dug, find another sensible adult figure to whom the recalcitrant teenager will listen. There's almost always someone.

Herb: Much the same can be said about the ability to form opinions. It's important that young people have the space and encouragement to develop their own views and express them, in the knowledge that these, too, will most likely change many times. There is an added dimension, however, as we discuss in Chapter 9: the era of 'post-truth', when large online communities can reinforce views to the extent that they become very difficult to dislodge. Some of these opinions can be dangerous, from conspiracy theories to fundamentalism and fanaticism. MRI scans show that political and non-political statements have different neural activities, with the former more difficult to shift. Opinion should be formed by listening and observing, then thinking about it, then discussing, and only then deciding and acting if needed.

Tony: This is a process well worth discussing as a parent, because we all tend towards hasty actions based on little thought and a rewriting of the past. It's not easy to put into practice.

Herb: A few words about borderline personality disorder (BPD). This is not always easily recognized, and often misdiagnosed as depression. It has several clear-cut features, such as explosive anger, fear of abandonment, unstable relationships, self-image problems, marked impulsivity, mood swings and a tendency to self-harm among other features. BPD is now referred to interchangeably as emotionally unstable personality disorder (EUPD). It is well described on the MIND website, together with suggestions of help available. It's best to seek professional help, certainly at the outset.

Tony: There are many different personality characteristics. We can come across difficult or unpleasant individuals, for example, whether in the family or in school. Indeed, the phrase 'dark traits' is now an accepted term.

Herb: It's used in a recent University of Copenhagen study. These 'dark traits' include the so-called Dark Triad: psychopathy, narcissism and Machiavellianism. The authors also note sadism, spitefulness, egoism, self-interest, feelings of entitlement and other undesirable developmental characteristics which frequently overlap with one another. Those concerned are almost always able to justify their actions because of long-established belief systems. Without having to be professionals, we all tend to recognize people we know who exhibit traces of these personality groups. They might or might not have some insight into the way they are viewed by others, but professional help is only possible with those who genuinely want it.

Tony: And what do parents do with an unwilling teenager about whom they have concerns?

Herb: Good question. The only way some progress is possible is if this is felt to be an enduring personality trait; for many it is only temporary. If it's disturbing at home and elsewhere, then parents should arrange for an initial consultation with or without their child. I've seen this happen many times. Picture a distraught parent without the cause being present. I feel it important to stress that this affects everybody, so as to remove the idea that everything going wrong is the child's fault. Parents have a better chance of including all children at future meetings if it is clearly spelt out that this is a family matter which needs to be sorted out together.

Tony: One problem I have encountered is parents who leap to the assumption that their badly behaved child must have some personality disorder. Usually this is not the case. It might be an example of testing behaviour, perhaps in extreme form, like the boy who doused himself with petrol for a dare: a worrying incident, but the kind of thing an adolescent might well do. Adults have to do the right thing and respond appropriately (laying down the boundaries), but not overreact. On the one hand, passive acceptance is harmful, and may well worsen the situation in the future, but on the other, any sanction must be pitched at the right level following reasonable discussion.

PARENTING STYLES

Herb: With this talk of traits and styles we should consider the way parents behave as well as children. There are many classifications of parenting style, but there are four basic ones recognized by most professionals: neglectful, permissive, authoritarian and authoritative. Inevitably there are overlaps between these at different stages of development as a result of changes of relationship between parents and children, such as divorce, illness and just the passing of time.

Tony: I admit I have tended to define parenting styles only when I believe parents are getting it conspicuously wrong, such as the Velcro (stuck to the child), Helicopter (forever hovering), Lawnmower (constantly preparing the ground) and the Bulldozer (sweeping all before in order to create a clear path with no obstructions). I accept there is a more balanced way to look at it! The *neglectful* parents must be the worst.

Herb: They are, but overlaps are even worse: neglectful authoritarian, for example. Such neglect can cover every area of growth and development. In this setting there are poor lines of communication, the physical and emotional needs of the children are overlooked and ignored, and the child is at risk, not necessarily because parents wish to be damaging to their children. They may well have experienced similar upbringings, and respond to support and guidance. This kind of parenting tends to be associated with the most impoverished of circumstances, but can be witnessed in every social class.

Tony: That's indeed the case, but there are other dimensions of neglect that seem to me particularly bad: if parents are away from home excessively and no information is given to children; when they have no interest in what is happening at school (even if, in some cases, they are paying a great deal of money for it); where no attention is given to a child's friends; when parent-teacher meetings are always missed and there is little knowledge of their children's whereabouts. This is the worst kind of parenting. Sometimes it's shockingly deliberate, but more often it is born of parental busyness and self-absorption in their own lives. They really need help, but reaching them can be hard. It can take some hard conversations with a teacher or a friend for them to see the damage being done to their children.

Herb: The *permissive* parent, by contrast, is over-indulgent, allowing young people to get away with virtually anything because parental expectations are low. Overwhelming leniency causes real harm. This is essentially an unstructured household in which young people have no need to develop self-control and self-discipline or think of others, with the problems spilling out into all aspects of their lives, possibly even including future parenting.

Tony: What you describe as permissive parenting is much more common than it used to be. I come across parents who seem to be in constant fear of doing something that might make their child no longer love them, whether it's tamely allowing unfettered access to the internet, smoking cannabis at home, going out at night with neither permission nor comment, or just tolerating aggression. This attitude is often driven by a desire to be the teenager's friend. Liberally distributing alcohol from the boot of a car at a cricket match, for example (with catastrophic results). Leaving aside the fact that good friends don't simply roll over and give in, the last thing teenagers want is their parent as friend, any more than they want a matey teacher. Parents have a role to play, and a crucial one at that.

Herb: We have long understood that feelings of safety derive from the secure knowledge that there are boundaries which are comforting. In the long run role-blurring and rule-breaking don't make for either happy parents or children. Young people in this group are more likely to get into trouble, have fewer social skills, be less motivated academically (because there is always praise from parents whatever the outcome), and have difficulty with authority figures away from home – because they can always count on the unconditional support of their parents. They see themselves as the centre of the universe – which to some degree they are, at least at home.

Tony: At the other end of the scale there are the *authoritarian* parents, who control family life tightly. Rules are cast in stone and not open to discussion or revision. Infringement may well lead to punishment which may be physical even in this day and age. Sometimes these can be emotionally cold households, but not always. One charming, if feckless, 15-year-old boy had an equally charming father who would present his son with a typed itinerary for each day of the holiday at home. The boy was under orders, and not allowed to exercise any choice. His days ran on rails. Small wonder that school for him was release, but he was singularly unable to direct himself, even simply to arrive at the right place for a lesson, let alone be on time.

Herb: Children in these households are apprehensive about exploration or original thinking because they fear possible punishment. They are insecure in social settings, self-esteem is low and they are often shy and withdraw from groups. They tend to have a rather binary approach to the world, responding to situations very differently within the structured family and outside it.

Tony: Which brings us to the last of these broad categories, the *authoritative* parent, who is likely to be the most rewarding and beneficial type.

Herb: That's because there is understanding in the family that a child has a series of developmental stages and of what these are. There are also high expectations about the quality of relationships between all members of the family, as well as a willingness to create opportunities for individual development.

Tony: Effective families such as you describe seem to share particular ways of functioning: reasonable expectations according to age and development, rules with consequences, good communication and encouragement of reasoned opinion being at the heart of it.

Herb: Yes. That's a hallmark of success. It's just that the conditions in which to bring up a family are more challenging than ever before, which is why there are more points of reference outside the family offering support: witness a raft of websites like Parentline, Young Minds, Positive Parenting and Mumsnet.

Tony: Tougher it may be in some ways, not least because much of what a child experiences today is unfamiliar to a parent's generation, but we cannot escape the fact that parental role models really matter, arguably more now than ever. We all have our own distinctive parenting style, whether we know it or not. We serve our family well by taking a cool look at what we're doing.

ADOLESCENT TRICKS OF THE TRADE

Tony: There's a lot of pressure on parents, the vast majority of whom want to do the best for their children. We've probably added to the pressure by talking about parenting styles! We can at least offer a toolkit as some kind of help, a way of looking at some of the predictably unpredictable behaviour we see in adolescents – their tricks of the trade.

Herb: These are known professionally as adolescent mechanisms. It is a common experience to have arguments about pocket money, homework, bedtimes etc, with children often citing friends who, it is claimed, have a much better deal. These arguments are part of a natural testing-out process.

What follows is our list of some of the most commonly observed ones, which are, in the main, part of the process of coming to terms with growing up. Our top tricks of the trade:

Moods

It is simply impossible to have any discussion about adolescence without bringing up the horrors of grumpiness, moodiness and oppositional behaviour. The wonderful child morphs into an unpleasant, messy, uncaring, angry/silent, rule-breaking tyrant, unpredictable and sometimes frightening, especially as physical strength and size increase. Family values are challenged.

'You hate them and they hate you,
They hate themselves and others, too.' (Herb)

Parents can take some comfort in the knowledge that the impulse-control and decision-making parts of the brain have yet to develop fully, but knowing this does not always take the sting out of dealing with frustration, threats and withdrawal.

Aggression

This is more common in boys, but increasingly girls are doing much the same things. Features include bullying, fights, vandalism and lack of remorse. Bad external influences are difficult to detect, and become more problematic when suspicions are voiced which are interpreted as interfering in their lives.

Unpredictable behaviour
When teenagers become preoccupied with self-image, perceived attractiveness dominated by bodily shape and the onset of sexual feelings, it triggers a sensitivity and vulnerability which can express itself in sudden unexplained hostility and mood swings.

Splitting
Playing off one parent against another should not be tolerated. It can be a disaster for all concerned, not least the child in terms of developing personality. Some methods of splitting are pretty obvious, others more subtle, and require subtlety in response. While it is the relationship between parents that is most often exploited, splitting can happen between siblings, and between school and parents; every case needs to be countered and not allowed to take root.

Testing out
Testing is a critical process, but not necessarily always a conscious thing. Common features and examples relate to 'How much can I get away with?'; 'How effectively will adults cope with my response?'; 'Are they being consistent and fair?'; and, importantly, 'Will I get much the same reactions from all other adults around me?' In similar fashion, testing is very common when teenagers face a new teacher.

Levelling
This is another interesting phenomenon, when a teenager takes advice and models him- or herself on an adult or

authority figure either within or outside the family, and feels equal as a result. This intuitive attempt to cast everyone as equal creates a perception that no one is better than they are. Actually, some distancing by significant adults is healthy, and is in fact much more supportive and influential than seeking to be 'good friends'.

Saint-like goodness

Some adolescents display a degree of compliance that can be disastrous for them in the long term. Being over-praised with comments like, 'Why can't the rest of you be like Johnny?', both at home and school, leads to unrealistic feelings of self-worth and distancing from other teenagers, who regard that individual as a 'goody-goody'. As self-enforced perfection wears thin and disillusionment follows it becomes something of a ticking time-bomb. In extreme forms it can lead to distancing, with the avoidance of contact, and even to a disconnected, dreamlike state.

Risk-taking

This is not so much related to age as to the variable growth of self-regulating mechanisms. It is a biological process and not readily susceptible to change by educating, essentially activity without thinking across every sphere of life. Sensation-seeking and novelty predominate, and attitudes to consequences have yet to develop; potential loss of face with peers also becomes a significant factor. A stimulus to risk-taking is the heady cocktail of fear and excitement. This cocktail is attractive to humans throughout life: witness gladiatorial combat, bullfighting, fast car racing and parkour. The thrill of success is heightened by the possibility of disaster. With adolescents these emotions are intensified. They underline the potency of gambling, drug-taking, certain sexual behaviours and the role of gangs.

Mischief

Included here to lament its passing. Low-level naughtiness and high spirits are wholly natural parts of growing up, and should be dealt swiftly and sensibly, and then move on. And even celebrated in schools – up to a point! Contemporary culture seems to demand that any small infringement is elevated to some formal level of sanction and labelling. This is counter-productive and damaging in itself. Let mischief live!

WHEN FUNDAMENTAL THINGS CHANGE: PARTING OF THE WAYS

Tony: We all have to cope with separation and loss throughout life. It's a fundamental part of human existence. There are other family dismemberments that affect adolescents profoundly, such as moving home, chronic illness, a parent's loss of job or status, imprisonment, even the loss of pets, but after bereavement of a loved one, the most consequential for adolescents is the divorce and/or separation of parents.

Herb: In terms of divorce and separation, there are probably three types of parting of the ways: the good, the bad and the indifferent. Inevitably there will be overlaps between them at different times, and what might seem good initially might turn out to be very bad indeed, or vice versa.

Bad separations are acrimonious, self-obsessed affairs during which children are collateral damage. *Indifferent* is when the children are grown up and have their own lives and the couple has just grown apart over time. The best are those couples who elect to remain friends leading separate lives, and who have spoken sensibly with their children over a period of time to allow them to adjust to a new reality: they have done their best to think through the implications for their children practically and emotionally. That's *good*.

Tony: There are some situations where divorce has positive features: for example, when a child has been a regular, helpless and often terrified spectator at open warfare between parents. That said, family breakdown has a major impact, and is often damaging to children of any age, and the way the change is handled will have a profound effect on their future.

Herb: Break-ups are a major problem irrespective of age, race, gender or social class. There's potential for closer relationships with other members of the family, but also significant estrangements, because taking sides is such a feature, and only too often expected of the children as well.

Tony: Children of all ages in the family home are likely to wonder if the divorce or separation is their fault, and if there's something they could or should have done to prevent it. At a time when identity is a fragile thing anyway, the adolescent is particularly vulnerable to these feelings. What strikes me is that all the acrimony and shouting rarely makes them have feelings of hatred to one or other parent. Mostly, they want some peace, to allow them to get on with their own lives. Parents who give some stability and calm to their children, whatever is going on, do them a great service. Schools and counsellors can be left picking up the pieces when they don't.

Herb: This is an important point. You lead me on to the unpleasant issue of Parental Alienation. Some children are turned against one parent by the other to the extent that they are led to say they wish to have nothing to do with the non-resident one. The parent who has custody will not have encouraged any contact with the other – in fact, in many cases, quite the opposite. This inevitably generates feelings of guilt and difficulty in expressing deep emotions. Years later, there will be anger and frustration at having been forced to practise divided loyalties and make a choice for the sake of peace.

Tony: Family breakdown is often cited as a cause of social problems. Given the range of family circumstances, this would seem rather simplistic.

Herb: The fall-out from instability and family collapse plays an inevitable role in the social ills of any society. As far as children are concerned, these include absconding, drug use, homelessness, the possible end to formal education, and mental health issues which might have been at least contained by some semblance of family togetherness. Even if support through the family was weak, having it withdrawn makes young people feel cast adrift.

Tony: When we look at a national, indeed international, picture, family breakdown certainly seems to be a modern norm. Britain has double the OECD average of 15-year-olds who do not live with both parents, and one of the highest rates in the EU of struggling single parents.

Herb: Breakdowns in the UK have actually reached epidemic proportions. Ten per cent of 16- to 24-year-olds are recorded as spending a month or more just 'sofa surfing' because of relationship failures, though not always family-based. What's alarming is the acceptance of and resignation about family collapse. And removing the fault clause from divorce proceedings could make it worse.

Tony: Why so? Removing the fault clause seems a thoroughly good thing. It should reduce some of the acrimony.

Herb: The easier divorce is to put into practice, the more likely it is to take place, often without careful planning and forethought. There was a huge rise in divorce after the 1971 reforms, and it will increase again with the further easing of barriers, vows and promises. As almost half of all marriages in this country end up with divorce already, family breakdown will become all the rage. Acceptable for adults, perhaps, but simply awful for the children involved.

Tony: I take your point about hastiness, but anything that helps to lead to a sensible, calm decision, especially when it involves children, must be positive. Would you advise parents with children at home to stick together pretty much no matter what, providing there is not open warfare in front of the children? Or do you accept the mantra that a personally fulfilled parent outside the home is better for the child?

Herb: How can we possibly argue with the idea that parental happiness is good for children? However, treating divorce in a casual fashion is self-indulgent. I remember one couple saying in front of their children that they could always remarry if the divorce didn't work out as anticipated! Go figure!

Tony: Let's turn the clock back. When parental breakdown first becomes a possibility, openness with children at a relative early age can only be to their advantage in the long term. It's a tough call when there is turmoil in a relationship, but insufficient information can be very damaging, and should be dealt with if at all possible in a way children can understand.

Herb: Preparing children for the inevitable, with some expectation about why it is happening, helps to prevent two things: feelings that they might be responsible in some way, and reunification fantasies – the false belief that it will all go away and everybody will be happy ever after. Older adolescents, in particular, can feel that their views and emotions are not taken into consideration insofar as residence and future ways of operating are concerned. A practical issue for a parent can run very deep with a child: moving schools at short notice, for example. The best advice is to give as much information as you feel your child can cope with. It isn't easy: too much information to children who are too young to process it adds to their distress.

Some points to remember when separation will dramatically affect family life

1 Couples living together, whether married or not, should seek some kind of mediation from family, friends or a professional before taking such a life-changing step for all concerned. Parents owe this to their children.

2 Be as open as possible as soon as possible, doing your best to pitch the information in a way that will be understood.

3 Encourage discussion, involving extended family and friends if that is helpful and they don't take sides.

4 Listen to children's concerns, some of which may seem minor to you in the scheme of things, but matter.

5 Repeatedly affirm your love for your child. In the case of divorce, both parents should do this equally.

6 Never undermine your other half in the eyes of the children.

7 Ensure that future contact with the non-resident parent is accepted by all as absolutely essential. If at all possible, avoid frightening, psychologically damaging open hostility.

8 Consistently reassure children that the new arrangement will work well, and give examples of other families who have succeeded in similar circumstances.

WHEN FUNDAMENTAL THINGS CHANGE: LOSS AND BEREAVEMENT

Tony: Death is inevitable, and at all ages the most distressing psychological phenomenon we experience, but there is some evidence that modern society deals with aspects of death less effectively than in past generations. It's one of the salutary experiences of a life spent in boarding schools that one appreciates the fragility of life. It's not just the impact of the deaths of older family members on adolescents, but the way they have to some to terms with the death of people within the school community, particularly their peers. Over my four decades in schools, in about one year in three the school had to deal with the death of a pupil, from all manner of causes, from a road traffic accident to cerebral malaria. Modern society has tended to sanitize death, which makes it harder to address.

Herb: The death of a loved one is traumatic. From a psychological point of view, death is best dealt with by demonstrating its finality. This means even young children, let alone adolescents, taking part in funeral and religious ceremonies to eliminate the possibility of troubling fantasies in the future. Primitive cultures have always accepted this finality, as should we.

Loss of a parent is more common than you might think: about 5 per cent of children in developed societies lose a parent during childhood or adolescence. Bereavement is tough at any time, but for adolescents what happens is that the whole process of personality development, the sense of self and identity, is cruelly interrupted. Many of the normal difficult changes which take place in adolescence can shift direction and be expressed in unpredictable ways. A great deal depends on the nature of the death: how unexpected and in what circumstances.

Tony: The most evident reaction in the case of a sudden death seems to be guilt, bringing with it a sense of unfinished business – 'I wish I had said . . .' – coupled with a desire to do something that at least has the semblance of being permanent.

Herb: Some therapists suggest both a guilt- and a wish-list, perhaps seeking to perpetuate memory through raising money for a relevant charity or volunteering to help at a hospice.

Tony: The ritual of death is important. In some ways teenagers seem rather better at dealing with this than adults. The most powerful and affecting words I have ever heard spoken at a funeral or memorial service have come from the young, with little artifice and a lot of heart. Occasions like this matter for all of us, but particularly children and adolescents. The idea that teenagers or even young children should be shielded from displays of grief is odd. There is a need for outpouring, just as there is for soothing.

Herb: A frequent reaction to sudden bereavement is a decline in academic performance, due to depression and anxiety which might be so extreme as to require individual counselling. Self-inflicted social isolation can be an issue as well. In most cases family structures are enough to offer care and support. A family should never shy away from seeking external support, which is a natural thing to do. In cases involving parental suicide or the sudden loss of both parents, professional help is essential.

Tony: I wonder if the effects are so different from traumatic divorce. Separation, guilt and anger are all there. In some ways it's worse, because there's a sense that divorce could have been avoided. In all these cases, the sense of loss can be profound.

CASE STUDY

Tony: This study from Herb's casebook illustrates some of the features we have discussed around divorce and the impact of fundamental change, but also touches on important themes in family life in general.

James presented as a pleasant, instantly likeable 14-year-old boy with a sad demeanour and a downcast expression. He had been referred by his parents, who were concerned at the fairly recent deterioration of his behaviour at home, though it was described as exemplary in all other settings.

The family consisted of two happily married individuals, both with good jobs and a positive outlook in almost all respects. The 16-year-old daughter was no concern at all: all the problems in a previously happy family seemed to be laid at James's door. This was made clear when the parents and their son were interviewed together, with James contributing very little during the initial discussion.

The history given was basic. Regarding themselves as a happy family with an excellent lifestyle, the parents felt it was their duty to share their blessings with someone less fortunate and privileged. Accordingly, they went through the proper procedures and fostered a boy of similar age to James. The first year went very well, with all three children getting along and Ed, the fostered child, rapidly settling into the family as one of their own. As all seemed so positive and to be going so well the parents had no hesitation in applying for full adoption, which was readily granted after a further year of fostering.

It was at this point that James's behaviour in the home became more turbulent and disruptive. This was unexpected and totally out of character. It became increasingly difficult for the other members of the family to cope with, and they felt wretched and out of their depth. Ed was particularly troubled, and began to feel distressed at the way his presence seemed to be the reason for the family tearing itself apart.

On his own, James confided in me that he had been very happy with everything that had happened in the two-year fostering period, until it became apparent that his mother was devoting more of her time to Ed than to him. When he challenged his mother in private, she explained very reasonably that Ed's life had been so unhappy and difficult before he became part of the family that his needs were greater than anyone else's, and he had to be the centre of her attention. Sister Milly seemed untroubled, and continued happily busy at home and school. She, too, however, was becoming fed up with James's tantrums and unpredictable behaviour and the way it was affecting family life. She had no problems with Ed, nor he with her.

Although it seemed very obvious to an outsider, no one, and particularly the mother, had been able to take on board the way in which James saw Ed's new position as displacing him in the family. What James found particularly distressing was the way his mother saw him as the guilty party in any of the usual brotherly arguments. 'After all, darling, you have to realize that Ed has had a terrible life, and now for the first time we are giving him what every child is entitled to. You have to make allowances, and try to understand why I am focusing so much attention on him: you have always done so well, and therefore don't need as much time and effort as you might have done when you were younger.' The conclusion was easy enough to draw. The situation was a major benefit to Ed, but for James it represented a loss of so much that he had taken for granted and was no longer available when he felt he needed it.

A few family sessions were required in order to reset the boundaries and enable understanding of what had taken place to be accepted and adjusted to by all concerned. Mother found it most difficult to understand and realign what had become her entrenched behaviour, but she took great pains, following guidance and suggestion and with the support of the rest of the family, to even out her approach to the two boys.

The problems James had in coping with the normal challenges, emotions and interpretations of adolescence had been greatly compounded by this distortion of the family dynamic. A subsequent follow-up meeting revealed his outlook had become much more positive.

EMPATHY

It used to be thought that empathy is a faculty which only develops fairly late in adolescence. It is essentially an ability to understand and share feelings. It's now, however, believed that its development can start at a much younger age, and not necessarily following the examples set by parents. Older siblings who are warm and have caring friendships, who are seen as supportive and kind, form good role models for their younger brothers and sisters. It seems to be a two-way development. This is not the same as understanding and showing sympathy, which does not include the concept of identification with someone else's emotions.

SIBLING RIVALRY AND BULLYING

Recent studies suggest that these family issues may lead to the development of psychiatric disturbances in older life, even such serious ones as psychosis. Both victim and offender may well suffer in consequence, particularly if parents or others do not pick up the problem sufficiently early. As is now generally appreciated, verbal bullying can be significantly more damaging than physical. It is not at all easy to know what to ignore and when to intervene, but instinct is usually the best guide. The important thing is that no one gets off scot-free when continual and severe bullying is a family dynamic.

WINNICOTT AND BETTELHEIM

A reassurance from two major experts in families and parenting: more than adequate parenting can be provided by the good-enough parent. In the 1950s Donald Winnicott wrote about 'good-enough mothering'. Thirty years later Bruno Bettelheim updated the idea as 'good-enough parenting'. Both men worked extensively with families, and their books make for good reading even now, notwithstanding all the changes in society. Essentially, 'good-enough parenting' takes away the burden of perfection, and revolves around ensuring that adequate attention has and is being paid to the young person's needs, physically, emotionally, socially and even spiritually.

WHAT ADOLESCENTS MOST NEED FROM ADULTS

Cultural behaviour and expectations can make the experiences of adolescents around the world seem very different: there are indeed different ways of viewing gender roles, for example, or the use of alcohol, or family duty. Yet when it comes to what adolescents most want from the adults who are significant in their lives, there is a remarkable commonality. From Shanghai to Chicago, Delhi to Durban, adolescents express very similar impulses and needs: they want honesty and trust.

This may seem an elementary statement, but it is striking how frequently adults are blind to the obvious, particularly when it comes to their own children. These qualities may seem self-evident, but they are too often side-lined.

Honesty

Adolescents, teenagers in particular, can sometimes seem slippery, loosely acquainted with the truth, so it may seem rich to hear from them that they want honesty from their parents and teachers. The internet is awash with advice about how to teach honesty to teenagers: we are told that they are self-absorbed and need non-judgemental parents to act as 'emotion coaches' and not as judges; they can be taught the 13, or 6, or 20 ways to inculcate honesty, from sounding board to values discussion to 'having it out', but what tends to be ignored is a simple, glaring truth. What matters most is parent as role model.

The word 'honesty' can mean different things to different people. Who decides what is honest? Strong moral or religious belief can offer a kind of certainty, but for most people honesty is not a boxed-up, static thing: it's fluid, and responds to circumstances. But it only works if it's rooted in underlying, unaltering truths. Adolescents are often very sensitive to what they see as adult hypocrisy, particularly at home.

Trust

In the adolescent mind, trust comes from boundaries, consistency, adults not telling outright lies, and feeling that they have a say. In the middle teenage years, in particular, young people really need clarity. As we have noted, they have a propensity to see things in black-and-white terms. Grey areas can confuse and lead to a loss of faith. Allowing a child to smoke cannabis at home and then sending him to a school with a robust drugs policy is setting him up for collision. Indulging poor behaviour with a smile and a shrug is short-changing a teenager. Not explaining (thoroughly and repeatedly) why a situation has to be this way, even if it seems unfair, is sowing confusion that undermines trust.

Teenagers often react badly to feeling that their parents are superior beings who impose unreasonable standards or expectations. Sometimes teenagers are right, but they can react with an aggressive superficial certainty which needs handling. Slapping down an apparently ridiculous assertion can fuel mistrust. Better to discuss and examine, time-consuming though this can be.

Some parents find it hard to say, 'I don't know the answer, but it seems to me . . .' Yet coming to terms with imperfections – of logic and emotion, their own and their parents' – is a crucial part of growing up healthily, and needs to be nurtured.

5

Sexuality

Tony: As fully rounded human beings we need a moral compass and a sense of purpose: we also need a coherent sexual identity. One way or another, sexuality matters hugely to all human beings: given the way sex is publicly expressed nowadays, perhaps more than ever.

Herb: Even before the onset of puberty, children display intense interest in what they perceive to be the sexual differences between male and female, mother and father. The Freudians and others have written an enormous amount about the extent to which attraction to the parent of the opposite sex is a feature. Even in the pre-teen years, parents observe more often than not the way in which their children are changing. Boys become very interested in mothers' sexuality, by focusing on her attractiveness, touching and looking at her breasts and so on, and possibly asking embarrassing questions, while girls become seductive and flirtatious with their fathers.

Tony: Yet by the time I see them in secondary school, boys and girls have erected strong psychological defences, whatever their deeper feelings may be.

Herb: Sexual behaviour in young to middle adolescence isn't the same as it is later and in adulthood. At this stage, children can easily be aroused, indeed, possibly too much, which can be very embarrassing, particularly for young boys (for obvious reasons), but in the early phase without any desire in the conventional emotional sense. Desire develops rather later, and leads to behaviours with or without the presence of the same or opposite sex. It is part of the process of experimentation. All of this is very much influenced by the way in which the sexes are portrayed in everyday life, from advertisements to television programmes to the cinema and so on.

Tony: The influences being brought to bear on young people when it comes to their sexuality are much greater than they used to be. In the past it was pretty normal to get information from parents or sex talks at school or, more commonly, from friends who seemed to be in the know, but this is no longer the norm. The advent of search engines and the omnipresence of tablets and phones allow young people to learn far more about sex in a disorganized and sometimes exaggerated and distorted way than used to be the case. Learning about sex has always been rather a random business, at least in Western society, but it's now chaotic.

Herb: We're looking at the changes in secondary sex characteristics (breast development, muscular growth, voice changes and so on) at the beginning of what nature intended as preparation for parenthood. The changes are not only physical and obvious, but emotional and social, too. Important here is the apparent fact that levels of hormone activity certainly affect sexual feelings of arousal, but don't necessarily lead to one route for everybody;

this would be far more dependent on the many variables already incorporated into their psychological development, and also those determined by social factors around them in both family and peer group.

Tony: Sex is sometimes portrayed as though there's an overriding biological need, especially for boys, to have a physical sex act with someone else in order to experience pleasure and release tension. It's presented as if it's an urge from our earliest sexual awakening.

Herb: Which is not the case at all. Boys start playing with themselves and masturbating in the early teens, or perhaps even well before that, to some extent in order to assure themselves of their masculinity. They are not that interested in girls, although there might be some fantasy elements involved. Comparison with other boys is the big thing, as is experimentation. This is most comfortably undertaken in an all-male environment, and almost always with teasing, embarrassment, laughter and some suppression of genuine feelings. By the age of 18, more than 80 per cent of boys bring themselves to orgasm, and do so three times as frequently as the almost 50 per cent of girls who do the same thing.

Tony: Masturbation is still seen as an aberration, even a sin, in some parts of society and around the world. Does this account for the 20 per cent of 18-year-old boys in the UK survey?

Herb: There are certainly religious and social constraints for some boys, and the influence of the immediate social group can be strong, but there are also some young people with low levels of response or, indeed, who are what is sometimes described as 'asexual'. Girls don't appear to require masturbation to the same extent as boys. Their initial sense of femininity develops at its best when there is a good adult male connection and male admiration. This could be from father, teachers, uncles or older cousins and family friends who are not seductive in any sense, other than making the girl feel good about herself.

Tony: Generally speaking, masturbation has come to be seen as more acceptable and healthy, but habits of fashion have changed in other ways, too. Oral sex was once seen as a particularly intimate and private thing, but now seems to be an initial point of sexual contact between young people.

Herb: Yes, oral sex seems now to be on a par with kissing and fondling: it is seen as safe. But it isn't. Sexually-transmitted diseases can develop through oral contact.

Tony: We're racking up a whole set of worries for parents, and we have yet to speak about role models. Both sexes have always had fantasy individuals, such as actors, sportsmen and sportswomen, popstars and older individuals, whether or not of the same sex, on whom they attempt to model themselves in dress, speech, mannerisms and even attitudes. This has been natural and often harmless, but I wonder about the extent to which role models have become distorted in the Internet age when it comes to sexual behaviour. Young people who simply don't know enough about sex and its ramifications are vulnerable. When do you feel parents should first start talking to their children about sex?

Herb: That's a very interesting question, given that the traditional birds-and-the-bees talk seems to have faded into history. If teaching about the process is left to parents, only too often nothing is said at all. How different this is from so-called primitive societies, who have an approach that has been developed over many generations to inform and develop sexual roles in young people. Who are the unsophisticated here?

Tony: Much the same could be said about the approach schools take. We'll talk about that later.

GENDER IDENTITY

Herb: The phrase 'gender identity' is much in use these days. It means how anyone feels *personally* about where he or she falls in the gender spectrum. In most cases, it is the sex which is assigned at birth because there are obvious anatomical features. Sexual orientation is not necessarily the same thing at all. An additional dimension is 'gender expression', which refers to the way a boy or girl appears and presents, through voice, clothes, hair, manner and so on. Gender dysphoria is where there is confusion and uncertainty.

Tony: In a report written by Hannah Shrimpton, using the findings of an Ipsos Mori poll in July 2018, it's revealed that 66 per cent of young people aged between 16 and 22 describe themselves as 'exclusively heterosexual'. Thirty-three per cent do not. The statistics show that the youngest generation are 'being affected by more and open fluid attitudes. They have grown up in a time when gender is not a simple binary and fixed identity has been questioned much more widely. This is new, and affects wider views of gender, sexuality and identity'. The report shows that 3 in 5 British 15- and 16-year-olds think of sexuality as a sliding scale where it is possible to be somewhere in the middle. Are you surprised by the findings of this report?

Herb: Yes, I am. It's startling to see the shift in a relatively short space of time. It was only in 1967 that the Wolfenden act determined that homosexuality was not a criminal offence. While some obviously gay individuals were tolerated and largely accepted – people like Benjamin Britten and actors of his generation – presumably on the understanding that there was not too much display of their proclivities, many had a very bad time (one thinks of Alan Turing). And this was the relatively straightforward matter of homosexuality. The notion of gender fluidity would have been inconceivable.

Tony: We often use words gender and sex as if they mean exactly the same thing, but they don't. I take sexual identity as being anatomical –

Herb: – and assigned at birth by appearance, on the understanding that there is a specific chromosomal part of the individual determining the physical external appearance and, also, what goes on inside the body.

Tony: Whereas gender is a psychological social term involving an individual's own identification of where they belong in the spectrum.

Herb: Yes. Gender is a crucial part of one's identity: the feeling that one is a male or a female, or somewhere in-between. In other words, gender identity lies between the ears, and sexual identity is between the legs, to put it crudely.

Tony: Everyone is seemingly born one or the other physically, and combinations of the two are rare, as in hermaphrodites, but gender identity can be an issue even for quite young children, and be confusing not just to the individuals concerned but to those around them. At what age have you seen gender identity become a problem for families?

Herb: Earlier than you might believe. According to the Tavistock Centre in London, children as young as four have been among the recent record numbers who have asked the NHS for help in gender-related problems. Most of these are of mid-adolescent age, but some are much younger. The key change has been removing much of the stigma attached to discussion of sexual identity. This is perhaps one of the positive aspects of going online, where so much of this is discussed, accepted and even on occasions seemingly desirable! Some younger teenagers might be given hormones to delay puberty in order to assess what's really happening, although it is highly unlikely that the average family doctor would prescribe hormone blockers for anyone under the age of 16.

Tony: There's such turmoil about sexual identity confusion, especially with regard to younger children, that parents can be seriously perplexed and anxious. Not least, they can be worried about ideas being put into impressionable young minds by people with some kind of agenda. How should parents deal with it?

Herb: Neither encourage nor discourage: let boys play with dolls and girls with guns in order to find their own level at a later stage. And be low-key; don't make a drama out of it. This area is highly controversial at present, and being made increasingly confusing for young people by the machinations of the adult world around them. If all else fails, there is the option of referral to a specialist centre such as the Tavistock, where a full assessment programme can be undertaken and future actions decided. This could include hormone therapy from 16 and surgery at 18, if that was deemed appropriate following a full medical and psychological evaluation. There's an argument, though, that most people will have become pubertal before 16, and a change of gender psychologically is much more difficult thereafter. We have to recognize that chronological and developmental ages are not necessarily in tandem.

Tony: There are many ways people feel about themselves as sexual beings, with the vast majority of individuals regarding themselves as heterosexual. You mention a reduction in stigma, but for those who are not part of the heterosexual mainstream, it seems the biggest problem they face through the school-age years is how they feel or act or look, and the extent to which they will still, in fact, be bullied, stigmatized and isolated.

Herb: Coming from a headmaster, that is a sad admission for the 21st century, but it's changing in some areas.

Tony: We have to face up to the reality. I, too, have witnessed a significant change in the last couple of decades. In the right environment, young people can be open, supportive and encouraging when it comes to an individual situation: they rally round. Teenage herd instinct is a tricky beast, however. The same person who is supportive of someone they know can be crass and vindictive in name-calling when they are part of a group. As so often in schools, it is the group dynamic that needs addressing. The landscape of gender identity now seems to be moving all the time, and this can be difficult for schools, let alone parents, so it would be worth us trying to identify some reference points.

Herb: Sexual orientation is defined as the way in which an individual's arousal, both physical and emotional, is to another person (who may or may not be of the same or opposite sex), and does not imply that active sex of any kind is taking place.

Tony: That's a really important point for parents to understand: it's an emotional as much as a physical thing.

Herb: The three basic variants we have always used in the past were: heterosexual, when it is the opposite sex; homosexual, if it is of the same sex (male or female); or bisexual, if the attraction is to either sex at different times or permanently. Most have shifting alliances and attractions, particularly before the process of adolescence is complete, usually after the mid-20s. Young people who eventually believe that they belong to any of the above categories do not necessarily declare their status until they feel ready to 'come out', which implies that they have reached the stage where they feel a modicum of safety in doing so. There are many studies which offer similar outcomes in terms of percentages concerning the way in which young people feel. Most studies come from either the Americas or Western Europe.

Tony: Surveys about sexuality are themselves fluid and different. New and sometimes contradictory statistics seem to be thrown up in each one published. As a rule of thumb, most surveys tend to under-report the actual realities. The important thing is that there has been an openness and willingness to discuss sexuality in the last couple of decades which has marked a significant change.

Herb: Insecurities around gender identity can be the cause of much soul-searching, emotional uncertainty and stress. That many young people waver and find themselves constantly changing only adds to feelings of despair and confusion. It can be problematic for family and friends, too, who may be wondering, if someone is actually gay, what they should do about it. Superficial signs, such as a propensity to wear make-up, cross-dress or adopt a particular mode of speech, are not proof-positive by any means of sexual orientation. It is quite common to meet effeminate men who are happily married with children, for example. Despite the fact that an increasing number of well-known figures have 'come out' without the appalling condemnation or criticism to which they would have been subject only a few years ago, many public figures remain guarded about openness. It is a private matter, after all, and this should be respected. Being 'outed', for whatever reason, is a treacherous act.

Tony: It's not surprising that anyone should be guarded. The politics of gender identity can be bitter. The LGBT Pride march in London in July 2018, for example, faced an attempted hijack by a small, radical group called Get the L Out, which claimed to be promoting lesbian rights by attacking the trans movement because it was 'conservative' and 'reinforced sexist stereotypes'. Wheels within wheels. This kind of intolerance sets back the cause of an inclusive openness, be it for public figures or adolescents.

Herb: It's certainly a kaleidoscopically changing world. It might be helpful to define some terms (see box), but some of the terminology is likely soon to be out of date.

Tony: Notwithstanding all this complexity, the underlying message must be about openhearted generosity and acceptance of all human beings with their panoply of sexual difference. What should connect this apparently disparate array is simply respect for others.

SOME DEFINITIONS:

GENDER IDENTITY is a personal, internal, cultural and emotional process which may or may not be observed by the world at large. It is also a psychological perception which may or may not be anatomically as expected.

ANATOMIC SEX means definition by the obvious sex organs at birth.

INTERSEX refers to an individual born with sexual features which do not conform to typical medical definitions of either male or female.

TRANSITION is the way in which an individual behaves in order to display a gender identity completely different from that assigned birth. Transitioning from

---

male to female or vice versa has become increasingly accepted and understood, but it is not without its problems for those who subsequently feel they have a need to be DE-TRANSITIONED, either hormonally or even following surgery.

TRANS is an umbrella term describing a wide variety of people whose gender identities do not align with biological sexual ones. Examples are: TRANSVESTITES, who are not always gay, but like to dress in the clothing of the opposite sex; TRANSGENDER, denoting someone who may be born a boy but emotionally feels like a girl or vice versa. It is a gender identity issue which could be hetero-, homo- or bisexual.

GENDERQUEER tends to be a political stance taken against conformity of gender expectations.

QTIPOC refers to queer, trans or intersex individuals and people of colour.

TRANS-EMBODIMENT is the way in which people fully appreciate, celebrate and view their abilities.

GENDER FLUIDITY means being more aware of an individual's proclivities. It requires the abandoning of preconceived, traditionally held views about sexual stereotypes.

CISGENDERED is the way in which non-trans people align their gender identities with the biological identity they were assigned at birth.

BISEXUALITY is the desire and ability to be sexually connected with both the same and the opposite sex, but the incidence is very difficult to determine, because so many individuals do not tell the truth when questioned. It is much more common experimentally than believed, and can occur at any stage in life

All the above and other terms of gender identity are now in common use. Recently there has been a dramatic increase in the number and range of terms used to describe variants and sub-variants in descriptions of gender and sexuality. This is a complex area, with a great deal of overlapping which is confusing for professionals, let alone parents and adolescents.

LGBT were the original, fairly simple, broad areas which were easy to understand and, possibly as a consequence, to accept. In this acronym, L = lesbian, G = gay, B = bisexual, T = transgender and transsexual.

A little more up-to-date is the variant LGBTQQIP2SAAK. The new arrivals are: QQ = queer and questioning, I = intersexual, P = pansexual (attracted to someone regardless of gender identity: it is a rejection of labelling, even if pansexual in itself is a label!), 2S = two-spirit (regularly moves between two identities), A = asexual, A = ally (an individual who is not any of the above but is supportive nonetheless), K = kinky (people with unusual proclivities).

SOME CONSEQUENCES

Herb: It's probably fair to say that the very topic of sexuality becomes difficult even in this day and age for rather a lot of people to wise up to and discuss openly and honestly. It's even worse when we're talking about young people. An American study of almost 300,000 from the late 1960s ran for almost 40 years, as an attempt to determine what changes had occurred over that time. Following the sexual revolution of the 1960s, the average age at which a girl lost her virginity was 18. Only 30 years later, the average age at which this happened was 15.

Tony: A lot more is known at a much earlier age about sexual activity than ever before, as a consequence of television, small screens, advertisements, magazines and so on. It becomes a desirable option even for pre-teens. The problem is that they have a lot of information and ideas for which they are not at all adequately prepared. The physical ability to engage is already in place, but the emotional and psychological connotations involved are nowhere near as developed as they need to be.

Herb: That's certainly true. In talking to teenagers, it's clear that to them sex means full sexual intercourse. As far as professional people like you and me are concerned, any formal contact leading to sexual gratification should fall under that umbrella. This would include petting, kissing, mutual masturbation, oral sex and so on.

Tony: I have witnessed conversations between adolescents and middle-aged teachers who were using the same language about sex, but were talking at cross purposes. This can be confusing, not only for young people but also for those working with them.

Herb: Perceptions shift and change. It's interesting that while teenagers can categorize any activity other than full intercourse as 'not sex', I have noticed that the definition of being a virgin in females is not as clear-cut as it used to be. There have been lots of other physical interactions – often given a level of validation in pornography – such as an increasing incidence of anal intercourse, that are attempts to avoid pregnancy and to leave the hymen intact. Without becoming too specific, an intact hymen is often required in some societies in order to allow marriage to take place. It is actually looked for!

Tony: Teenage pregnancy is arguably less of an issue than some years ago – at least, the pregnancy rates have fallen dramatically.

Herb: It's still a concern, and we need to continue as a society actively to educate our boys and girls about the risks of pregnancy. Most teenagers seem to know they have to do everything possible to avoid it. Were this unwanted problem to arise, there is the potential aftermath of miscarriage, abortion, the actual birth itself leading to possible rejection, denial of paternity, DNA investigations and more.

Tony: I'm concerned about the broader psychological and social impact of a change in attitude to sex. I recently had a long conversation with a bright, articulate, 18-year-old boy. He described the casual, spur-of-the-moment, un-thought-through, often brief sexual activity that characterized the behaviour of his group – often, but by no means always, under the influence of alcohol or drugs. He took this behaviour as an unremarkable norm. Neither this boy nor girl friends had any intention of developing relationships through sex, which they saw as an isolated act in itself. He was happy with that. But he then went on to describe the lack of commitment his peers showed to anything. He bemoaned the failure of boys to honour commitments to football practice (he was captain of the team). Did he see the connection? I asked. He pondered a while, and said he thought his friends often 'passed like ships in the night'. But neither he nor they would change.

Herb: My immediate concern is a more physical one. While unwanted pregnancy is a headline issue, more sinister is the prevalence of sexually transmitted diseases (STDs)

SEX EDUCATION

Herb: Do you think schools have failed, as far as ensuring children know all about the biology of sex, and the pleasures and pitfalls of sexual relationships? Despite more information being discussed in the classroom, it's surprising to discover that more and more young people are relying on YouTube etc, with all its unpredictability, rather than what they have learnt in school.

Tony: I think that's a little harsh on schools. The quality of formal sex education has improved over the years, but it's necessarily limited. Schools should only be one part of the equation. The recent move by the UK government to include relationships with sex education (RSE) is a good step forward. This compulsory course includes information about the basics, but also deals with the dangers of pornography, sexting, cyber-bullying and so on. Quite properly, parents' views matter. A problem, however, is that parents have the right to withdraw children from this course, without due regard for the consequences, which can leave some young people adrift and exposed, with the internet as the only source of information privately available to them. That said, it's natural for young people to be curious about sex and find any means possible to discover more. The internet is another way to do that.

Herb: It seems to have reached the point where almost all kinds of sexual education are derived from the Internet. The fears and misgivings that young people have are much more easily dealt with by tuning into one or other of the many 'experts', and who is to say that they are wrong to do so. There are British vloggers and American ones: Laci Green in the US is said to have well over one and a half million subscribers discussing all manner of things to do with sex.

This phenomenon has extended to other countries around the world. It can deal with questions and fears about LGBT, consent, open relationships and many other anxieties which are difficult if not impossible to talk about in group settings such as classrooms. One benefit is that advice is instantly available as anxieties arise. I see nothing salacious in this at all. As long as information is taken from more than one source and corroborated, young people can usefully educate themselves. Most are intelligent enough to examine many sources of information.

Tony: Healthy scepticism, if not there already, should be taught: a high index of suspicion is necessary. Triangulating sources of information is a recurring theme when it comes to dealing with the internet and the young. The first, basic, sound source of information should be school biology, which sounds straightforward enough, but if this relatively safe area is dealt with in a ham-fisted way by teachers, it can leave young people more anxious than they were before. It's not easy to get it right. I have watched a biology teacher put off a whole class of boys and girls by adopting a butcher's approach to meat. I have also seen teachers look embarrassed, even queasy. As a doctor, what would be your expectation of the teaching of human biology?

Herb: It should be matter-of-fact and factual, level-headed and non-judgemental. All these elements are needed. Young people need to be able to trust the information they are given and see it as relevant to their lives.

Tony: What age would you start teaching children about sex?

Herb: I'm reluctant to put a number on it, because adults should be responsive to children about sex at any age. The important thing is that adults should be honest, open and appropriately informative, taking the age and the intellectual/emotional capability of the child into account. I would give much the same answer to parents asking how to deal with the subject of death.

Tony: At the school end, I've encountered plenty of parents who have ducked the issue, but also an increasing number who have overburdened their children with information they don't need and which can actually cause them anxiety. What you call being 'appropriately informative' often means keeping it simple.

Herb: Very much so. When it comes to the relationships between adults and children in schools, what approaches, other than teaching biology in class, seem most useful to you?

Tony: The heart of it lies in some form of tutoring arrangement through which teachers can develop fuller relationships and higher levels of trust. This can be done face-to-face, or through small groups, or through an adroit use of resources with larger classes: each child in each school needs to feel connected to a responsible and responsive adult. That said, there's a surprising number of teachers who don't feel equipped to support children in this way. I remember a head of maths coming to see me to ask to be taken off all tutor arrangements because it was not 'his thing': he saw himself as a maths teacher in the classroom with no other expectations made of him.

Herb: How did you deal with him?

Tony: I explained to him why I thought this was a central role for all teachers, and that while we would go out of our way to understand his position, if he really didn't want to do it he was in the wrong school and, possibly, the wrong profession. To his credit, he responded to the challenge and we made some progress. We need teachers who are well trained and feel comfortable talking about sex in the context of relationships, which includes helping young people to have the self-confidence to say no, if they wish. This is altogether a different thing to teaching biology.

Herb: It seems that the role of the parent/carer/adult is now more important than ever before, but frequently they themselves can feel insecure. There are ways of finding help – for example, it's always possible to talk to one's doctor – but the barriers of embarrassment, and often the difficulty in getting an appointment, can prove insurmountable. What other routes of support would you suggest?

Tony: In the first place, I would look to family and friends who feel more secure talking about sex and other matters. Schools should have a counselling service available: at present this provision is patchy, but in time it will become the norm. It is also worth looking at GP practices which might have specialist nurses, clinical psychologists and in some cases social service support.

Herb: I would add the voluntary sector and official organizations like CAMHS. Then there are state agencies, as well as voluntary groups like ChildLine and, as we have discussed, the possibility of using 'virtual friends' on the internet, where caution should be the watchword.

SEXUALLY TRANSMITTED DISEASES

There has been a great increase in the incidence of STDs, sometimes referred to as STIs, (Sexually Transmitted Illnesses). Some, like syphilis, are regarded as historical. Infection does not require full sexual intercourse: petting, kissing and fondling can also cause STDs; pregnancy precautions don't ensure safety. Toilet seats don't usually transmit infections: unsterilized needles do! Some of the key conditions of which we should be aware:

Gonorrhoea and Chlamydia – now resistant to antibiotics. Major consequences for infertility and healthy pregnancy.

Herpes Simplex Virus – painful blisters in the genital area for both sexes. No definite cure. Can be asymptomatic, but still infect others.

Human Immunodeficiency Virus; HIV – responsible for acquired Immune Deficiency Syndrome (AIDS). Was at first invariably fatal, but now easily tested for and treatable, although incurable. Vaccines possible in the future, but concealment and infectivity are a criminal offence.

Hepatitis B and C – both cause liver disease with possible serious consequences. Hep B might disappear on its own, but Hep C can cause long-term difficulties, even though asymptomatic. Treatment is now available.

Human Papillomavirus; HPV – the commonest STD in young people. Often without symptoms, so easily spread. Causes genital warts and potentially cancerous in the mouth and genitalia. Precautionary vaccines should probably be given to all adolescents.

Trichomonas – a parasite in the vagina or penis. Treatable, but diagnosis is not easy until discomfort and itching become overpowering.

Syphilis – rife until penicillin arrived. Following a long quiescent period, the spirochete has developed resistance and is now back. First might present as a simple ulcer which heals itself, but the organism remains in the body causing damage to many parts, especially the brain.

Mycoplasma genitalium (MG) – not well known, but an increasing problem. Treatable with antibiotics, but resistance is growing. Burning sensation on urination and pain in the pelvis and lower abdomen are common.

Any anxiety, any symptomatology, or simply anything unusual in the genital region, means a trip to the doctor is essential. Medical professionals have seen it all before and are committed to confidentiality. However difficult it might be, parents need to advise young people to seek medical help at the earliest opportunity – and to encourage them to ensure sexual partners are aware.

Prevention is inevitably the best cure: be aware, know the facts and assess the risks.

COMING OUT

Tony: Feeling accepted as part of a social group is a natural human desire. In the teenage years this desire is often acutely felt. This is one reason why being open and honest about sexuality can be so difficult. Personal uncertainty can be aggravated by what a teenager perceives will be the reaction of others, especially from peers and parents. That said, there's a great deal of difference between 'coming out' and 'being outed': the former is voluntary and the latter is a kind of betrayal.

Herb: I imagine two people standing on the side of a very deep and cold lake. One is fully prepared to jump in, with wetsuit, good training, goggles, feeling confident and able to cope with what lies ahead – prepared for the consequences, real or imagined. The other feels naked and exposed, fearful of the cold, doubtful whether he or she can swim, crippled by uncertainty and the prospect of the hazards that lie ahead. The one pushed in is the one 'outed'. Whatever the motivation for the pushing, the outcomes can be the same: humiliation and misery.

Tony: Yet I've witnessed a sea-change in attitude in the West. When I listen to teenage boys and girls, their language is generally softer and more generous around sexuality than ever it was though, as we have observed, group behaviour can often be dismissive and even callous. The biggest change, however, is dealing with the individual who has the courage to speak up about his or her own sexual identity. In these cases, there is almost always a positive response in the mid- to older adolescent years, because friends and peers respond to the circumstances of the particular individual and can be very supportive, sometimes rather shaming the adults involved.

Herb: I think you're right to suggest that the issue is often more problematic for parents than for a teenager's friends. The adjustment for the family can be pretty tricky, and it's important for both parties to recognize that being sensitive to feelings and accepting the situation is both natural and normal. One piece of advice I give to parents about what *not* to say: when a young person comes out, parents may be tempted to say to them that they love them 'no matter what the situation might be'. This can readily be interpreted as suggesting that being gay is something abnormal or even abhorrent. It's better to say something along the lines of, 'I suspected it, and I'm grateful to know, and it makes no difference to the way I love you and always will.'

Tony: I recall one couple who felt that their two-year-old son was probably gay. They were relaxed about it, but said nothing to their son until he was a 15-year-old, at which point they gently asked him if there was anything he wanted to discuss about sexuality. Their son looked at them amazed and said that he had always known his parents knew he was gay and it was never an issue. He felt both loved and normal.

Herb: It's essential to stress that there is no such thing as a medical or psychological treatment to reverse gender identity. A person is what a person is. And their sexuality is really a very small element of how they will develop and relate to the world at large. I would also add that adjustment is greatly eased if the family in which it is happening has shown a warm and tolerant attitude in the past to the LGBT community. Any previous disparaging or hypercritical comments about others will inevitably make coming out for a child a very difficult process.

Tony: Have you had cases brought to you for conversion therapy?

Herb: Several. It's usually born of the attitude: 'Your problem is that you have not yet met Mr or Miss Right. When the time comes you'll be absolutely fine.' Clearly, not so. The therapy is better aimed at the parents who harbour that attitude. Convincing them of this was often a nightmare – they sometimes went elsewhere. Nevertheless, modern attitudes, the advent of Pride processions, news information, the voluntary coming-out of celebrities and many other factors have made this far less of a burden for the individuals affected, let alone the therapist!

Tony: The bigger problem I've witnessed is when a teenager is exposed to the glare of publicity without expecting it at all. This can be as a consequence of an honest and private discussion within a family reaching the ears of others; it can be much the same with a best friend in whom the teenager has confided. This can lead to immediate pain and embarrassment, even humiliation, but it also seems to have deeper consequences for the development of personality. I've seen boys and girls seriously messed up by what is, however well-intentioned, a breach of trust.

Herb: And it can be extreme. I have dealt with a number of boys and girls who experienced suicidal thoughts and even attempted suicide. This extreme reaction runs through all societies, and can be particularly acute in communities where very clearly defined and immutable restrictions around sexuality are in place. There are organizations available to help young people at such a critical point. One such is Befrienders Worldwide, which covers 29 countries and gives the appropriate support for the culture in which they are living. Another is Stonewall, and there is a growing number of supportive, useful websites offering practical advice.

PORNOGRAPHY

Herb: The availability of pornography even to very young children leads to a curiosity and interest that is not at all age-appropriate, and then to experimentation and physical stimulation without any real emotional preparation. In other words, children watch what is happening in front of them and gain a distorted idea of what human interaction is all about, never mind love and affection.

Tony: And yet pornography seems to answer some kind of human need. It continues to be the busiest activity on the Internet. Why do you think that is the case?

Herb: For a variety of reasons: fantasy, instant grati-fication, amusement, and because it has an addictive quality. Adults may choose what they wish for their entertainment (though the habit of using pornography has been shown to be ruinous in the lives even of some adults), but we should be particularly concerned for children and teenagers. Rather like very strong alcoholic drinks, pornography really isn't good for young people in terms of their developing brains and emotional well-being. It seems likely that any over-use in young people leads to the development of abnormal brain pathways with uncertain outcomes. There's a strong risk of a debilitating confusion: 'I am not the same as that. How can I pretend to be *that* way when I don't really feel it?'

Tony: It seems you are partly talking about young brains not having developed the ability to discriminate and self-protect, but it's also about immediacy and speed. Young people can bring the whole world to respond to the demands of their fingertips, and that sometimes means intense and frightening experiences which are at the same time fascinating. Nothing as delicious as forbidden fruit!

Herb: Porn online creates a normal or pseudo-normal awareness of what sexual activity is. There is none of the gradual working up to knowing more and more as time goes by as maturity ultimately develops. In the past the growth would be through discussion with friends, maybe access to magazines and books, and just the imagination. Today it's immediate and full on, and hard-core porn is just a click away. This tidal wave of instant pornography is a fact; part of our lives. You will have addressed this in schools over the years. What do you say to parents?

Tony: I acknowledge that, whatever well-intentioned restrictions are placed on access to porn, agile teenage minds will find a way around the blocks. So, in the first place, keep calm and don't overreact. Curiosity about sex is wholly natural. Open, level-headed conversation is the best way to ground this virtual experience into reality. Avoid being judgemental. If parents are genuinely concerned because behaviour they deem disgusting is repeated and conversation seems to have no effect, then professional help may well be required. Saying something along the lines of, 'We need help for both of us – we can't cope,' is a way to express concern as a family. Parents should never shy away from expressing how they feel, but place it in the context of an undimmed, supportive love. As always with teenagers, comment on their behaviour, not them as people.

6

Food

Herb: The most basic imperative in all living organisms, from amoeba to zebra, is to obtain nourishment in order to survive. Yet modern life, especially in the West, has huge issues with eating disorders. It seems an oxymoron, a self-inflicted wound. We have such a focus on intake, but too often take in too little of the right stuff, frequently a consequence of poverty and poor diets, and eat too much of the wrong stuff, leading to purging and vomiting. Eating habits are an accurate barometer of mental health and social values.

Tony: Eating habits have changed dramatically in my working lifetime. I have childhood memories of meals as set routines, both in school and at home. On the whole families sat down together, and some consideration was given to a balanced diet, although views about this have changed. In recent years more people, adults and teenagers alike, have eaten on the go. Life seems busier, and regular mealtimes have either fallen apart or become of secondary importance in growing up. Yet people and times change. Does any of this really matter?

Herb: It matters enormously. Young people need routines, and this is not just a question of a biological refuelling: mealtimes offer a nourishment that is emotional as much as physical. The mealtime is when family members can learn what is going on and what each other is doing, and comment and talk about their experiences. This ritual behaviour is now relatively uncommon. This is one respect where life in a residential setting, be it school, college or university, can have a distinct advantage for a young person.

Tony: It seems there is scarcely a magazine or newspaper these days that doesn't offer dietary advice of one kind or another.

Herb: This is partly in response to increasing obesity in the population, and also increased evidence of eating-based disorders, Diabetes 2 in particular, which is now becoming one of the most expensive areas health services throughout the developed world have to contend with.

Tony: What strikes me as a schoolteacher is the extent to which regular eating habits not only have a physical effect, but also impact the way the mind organizes itself.

Herb: It's a loss for the human experience that the fixed points of mealtimes have largely been displaced by other activities like watching TV – possibly one of the endless culinary programmes!

Tony: We've talked about some things that have been lost by different habits of eating, but usually when –

Herb: The word 'habit' is very important here, because habits give us continuity, and some awareness of predictability in our day-to-day lives.

Tony: Routines are a way of formalizing habits. One of my key messages to young people is that they are *liberating*. Embracing them frees up time to do other things. Routine gives a fixed point, in this case enabling the body clock to find a steady rhythm. Is this one-way traffic? Are there ways in which modern habits improve the situation?

Herb: Well, it's certainly true that good, nourishing food is more available in our society than ever before. Set against this, there are areas where children are not well fed. They may be given volume, but much of it may be of poor dietary quality, with an excessive emphasis on carbohydrates and sugars, which is exacerbated by eating on the move and by pre-bought food heated in a microwave with many additives, some potentially harmful.

Tony: What about the education of young people into good eating habits? When I was a head, relatively little time was formally given over to teaching about eating habits. There was oversight and informal conversation, and aspects of healthy eating were covered within the biology curriculum, but should this issue be a significant topic in its own right in schools?

Herb: This is an interesting question. Where do young people eat? At school? With friends? In the street? What is the quality of what they are eating in these various settings, and how should they learn what is good for them and what is not? Would they take any notice even if they were told?

The most important influence on most young adolescents is what their friends are doing. Very often, if there is an evening activity and a youngster goes out for a meal, he or she will leave as soon as possible to join friends and even eat again, in addition to what might have been lovingly prepared in the home. Is teaching what is good for you in terms of eating best done at home or from school? There are different approaches to the same thing: trying to inform them while not seeking to dictate to young people what is good for them in the long term. By whatever means, young people need to know that what they are eating now will have an impact on their future growth, their development and their long-term health. They need to understand their own machinery and how it is kept fit and effective, both physically and mentally.

Tony: So what practical advice can be given to parents about helping their teenagers adopt lifelong healthy eating habits?

Herb: At its most basic, feeding is loving, so the young baby gets security, stability and predictability from the breast and from the bottle at regular times and when needed. The nourished baby gradually develops into the young child and then the adolescent, when suddenly everything seems very different. Feeding at home is less important than it used to be, and one can say the same thing about the quality and quantity of food. When a young person either eats excessively at home or with friends or doesn't eat at all and is not very informative about where or she might be at any given time when meals are on the table, it can be distressing for parents.

Tony: From the social point of view, the evening meal traditionally and ideally has been a fixed point in the day when families would speak to each other. Given that that habit has largely disappeared and been replaced by the TV dinner or by nothing at all, what advice would you give parents about finding suitable times for a conversation?

Herb: Eating is nourishment, but eating together as a group is emotional nourishment as well. When this does not happen, families who do not get together frequently lose something deeply valuable.

Tony: So you are saying there is no compensation for this loss?

Herb: There is no compensation, because emotionality and the learning processes which are so powerful in family dynamics might be replaced by influences that may not necessarily lead to a healthy adulthood.

Tony: Eating together reinforces an emotional bond within the family, but does it also have a discernible effect on behaviour?

Herb: To a surprising extent, people who eat together tend to think and act in similar ways. We significantly underestimate the impact of mealtimes on emotional and mental health and social behaviour.

Tony: But most families are under huge pressure of time as well as other distractions, particularly social media. How much of a priority is mealtimes? How far should parents take the pain of adolescent irritation and rejection in order to sit around a table looking grumpily at each other?

Herb: All families have different ways of functioning. Routine mealtimes are most necessary with teenagers aged 14+ as pubertal phenomena are developing, especially with boys. It's easy for a teenager to break links with the family, rather harder quietly to return to the group, so it is a fight really worth having.

Tony: Apart from normal eating habits, the problem of eating disorders seems to be ever-increasing. In the indulgent Western world, obesity is on the rise, while in deprived, undeveloped regions hunger is still a distressing and seemingly relentless social problem in the 21st century. In those countries which have been developing very rapidly, particularly in the Far East, eating fads and eating disorders, which were once quite rare, are now rather dramatically on the increase, and are even regarded as a form of self-harm by some professionals.

Herb: Without creating a culture of suspicion, all parents and teachers should be aware of the possibility of an eating disorder. We will talk about tell-tale signs later on, but I cannot stress enough how important early diagnosis is in a successful outcome. A degree of honesty and self-awareness in adults is crucial, too, as you can see in the following case study from some years ago.

CASE STUDY

A 15-year-old girl was referred to my unit as a consequence of concern expressed both by school and parents about her physical state. Although she was not at a dangerously low weight she was exhibiting a reluctance to eat in the family environment. She never ate at school. The school was concerned about her general well-being, too: she was isolated from her peer group, had low self-esteem and feelings of worthlessness, and appeared to be in a depressed state.

She followed a programme of family therapy as well as individual and group therapy. During this time attempts were made to improve her self-esteem, build up confidence and teach her to be assertive within her family group. Throughout her period of treatment, it was clear that the family had very clear expectations which related to her social behaviour and her academic achievement. The parents were prepared to participate in family therapy sessions, but no clear shift in attitude could be perceived. They continued to wish to control the child's life and felt it was unreasonable that, as she matured from age 15 to 16, she should achieve greater independence.

The family view was that the girl's anorexia was a consequence of being unhappy at school. The girl supported this view. However, extensive liaison work with the school staff revealed they were concerned that the child was being pushed too hard academically at home. The family would not accept this, or that staff were acting reasonably in trying to persuade them to go easy on her. They felt that the school was solely responsible for any academic demands placed on the child. The parents would take no responsibility for having pressurized their child into academic achievement. Subsequently, the girl left the school and was transferred to another secondary school, where she continued to struggle with developing peer-group relationships and remained an individual with very low self-esteem.

EATING DISORDERS

Tony: It seems odd to talk about eating as a disorder. Eating disorders are an increasing concern these days, but they aren't a new phenomenon. Fads, picky eaters, fussy choices and lifestyle beliefs have become a normal part of modern Western living. It's not just a case of vegetarianism now, for example, but veganism, pollotarianism, pescetarianism, ovovegetarianism, lacto-ovo-vegetarianism and so on.

Herb: There is so much fluidity in the way in which individuals change their ideas that one of my own granddaughters is practising what one might label intermittentarianism – changing weekly according to circumstances. I see there is a new label for Food Neophobia (FN), which is a refusal to eat unfamiliar foods. And then there are intolerances and allergies. None of these are what I would call eating disorders.

Tony: From a school perspective, eating disorders are real enough. I have seen some truly awful cases, even leading to death. It's an area where parents and teachers frequently can feel completely helpless. I've seen how much boys can be affected as well as girls, developing an obsession with body-building supplements in place of a normal diet, for example. But there do seem to be an awful lot of myths. What are the facts?

Herb: The facts. Eating disorders can affect all ages and segments of the population, but it is teenagers who predominate among the approximately 1.25 million people in the UK who are affected. NICE (the national advisory institute for health and care) issues guidelines pointing out that the risk is highest in the 13- to 17-year-old age group. Girls tend to suffer more. About a quarter of cases are boys. Admissions to hospital for eating disorders generally have virtually doubled in the last six years according to NHS figures, and the number is rising. The current level is around 14,000, from mainly anorexia nervosa and bulimia cases, with almost a quarter of these the girls under the age of 18. Of course, these figures only capture reported cases. The actual number affected is likely to be much larger.

Early intervention is best for both the individual and everyone around him or her, but it is striking how often signals are missed or are ignored, sometimes because teachers and parents do not want to believe it. There are also practical problems, such as waiting times for outpatient appointments which can be as long as six months with child and adolescent mental health services.

BEAT, the eating disorders website, states that it takes three years on average for someone with an eating disorder to request treatment. The first port of call should be the general practitioner, but somebody has to be suspicious enough to push the young person forward in the first place. Self-referral is much less likely. Although hospital admission should be the last resort, the numbers involved have risen due to long waiting times for initial diagnosis and the worsening of symptoms as a result.

One of the troubles is that we seem to be pretty ignorant about the whole issue. A YouGov survey in 2018 noted that 79 per cent of adults were unable to name any psychological symptoms, such as low self-esteem or distorted perception of weight. BEAT notes that this is why treatment delay is such a frightening and potentially life-threatening issue. They offer six points to look for: obsessing about food, behavioural changes, distorted perception of body size, struggling to concentrate, rushing to the toilet after meals (to vomit, frequently silently and effortlessly), and excessive exercising. This sounds straightforward enough, but it isn't all that easy to pick up, as secretiveness and manipulation are more often than not part of the picture.

Another concern is teenagers who become obsessive about the *quality* of the food they eat, sometimes with alarming consequences. The medical term for this is orthorexia nervosa. It is not really professionally recognized as yet, but is descriptive and actually rather useful. Essentially it is when ritualized eating patterns of behaviour lead to restricted dieting, where there is a focus on the quality of food rather than the quantity. What starts off quite innocently as an insistence on eating no mass-produced food, avoiding all sugars, in the belief that gluten-free is best together with other organic food requirements, develops to such an extent that it can need professional intervention

Tony: It seems that pretty much any eating habit taken to excess will lead to problems. The best advice is surely as old as the hills: eat healthily and in moderation. A great deal of inherited wisdom still holds true, though it can be harder to see clearly in a world of burgeoning choice.

Herb: The trouble with simple advice, even if broadly true, is that it can suggest a simple solution. Eating problems are complex, and generally come under the title of FEDs: that is, feeding and eating disorders. There are four main types under this heading: anorexia nervosa, avoidant restrictive food intake disorder (ARFID), bulimia nervosa and binge-eating disorder. We will talk about these in more detail. Others included in this category are PICA (eating non-nutritive substances), body dysmorphic disorder (having problems envisaging one's own body shape), as well as other problems which are less significant in terms of volume. I cannot emphasize too much the importance of recognizing these as anything but do-it-yourself jobs. When something as serious as these arises, it is time for professional help, usually starting with a general practitioner with referrals to specialist clinics to follow.

ANOREXIA NERVOSA

Herb: Anorexia nervosa has been described as a weight phobia, a morbid fear of fatness and relentless pursuit of thinness – all of which are correct. The word *anorexia* comes from the Greek meaning absence of appetite. In fact, this is probably the least significant feature of the condition – indeed, is something of a misnomer, given that individuals with the disorder are frequently very hungry, and take pride in their ability to fight off the urge and starve themselves.

Tony: I've seen a complete range of anorexic and bulimic behaviour, from the seriously life-threatening to the merely over-conscientious dieter who has minor problems which are probably best left alone or ignored. Attending the funeral of a school pupil who has died as a result of a serious eating disorder really brings it home to you. We could do with some myth-busting here, too.

Herb: The diagnosis of anorexia is almost invariably made by someone else, rarely the patient. This means that whoever first sees the individual professionally has to deal with a very anxious parent accompanied by a sullen, resentful and often angry teenager who insists that there is actually nothing wrong with him or her, and is absolutely determined to present a picture of intelligent and active resistance. That is the situation with anorexia, less with bulimia, where fear of eating to excess can lead to the patient raising the issue.

Anorexia nervosa is increasingly diagnosed, and is most certainly not a new condition. The description provided by a physician named William Allbut in 1908 can hardly be bettered:

> the young woman thus affected, her clothes scarcely hanging together on her anatomy, her pulse slow and slack, her temperature 2° below the normal mean, her bowels closed, her hair like that of a corpse – tired, lustreless, her face and legs ashy and cold, her hollow eyes the only living thing about her; this wan creature, whose daily food might lie on a crownpiece, will be busy, yet on what funds God only knows.

Galen describes something similar in the second century AD, and Richard Morton in 1694 refers to it as a nervous consumption due to 'violent passions of the mind'.

Tony: We know that hunger and sex are the most basic drives in all animals. Man has sought to control these drives for a variety of reasons going way back in history and in most cultures. I assume there is some connection with anorexia, even if peripheral: the suppression of all appetites in a controlled way?

Herb: It would have been a precondition of celibacy. The concept of fasting leads to belief in purification of the body as well as the soul, given that it is used politically or to gain pity or as penitence or as purification or even a self-punishment – or combinations of all of these. It's interesting to speculate how far this self-denial links to the not entirely discredited notion that 'you are what you eat' –that is to say, diet is equivalent to personality. Mark Twain suggested that part of the secret of success in life is to eat what you like and let the food fight it out inside. That, alas, *is* discredited.

Body image is crucial in understanding anorexia. How big, tall, muscular, and fat or thin we think we are usually bears no relation to the way in which the outside world views us. Most of us have an homunculus: a miniature, fully-formed version of ourselves which resides in our brains and creates not just a self-image, but a sense of self-worth. In some cases this can be distorted, with a strongly negative view of body image which is related to discontent with life, depression and possibly mental instability, and increasingly with anorexia nervosa.

Originally anorexia nervosa was thought to be a form of hysteria, or even a type of schizophrenia. Some analysts actually regarded this as a symbolic rejection of the mother, interpreting the big tummy as impregnation! It has also been been seen, perhaps rightly, as a type of weight phobia, even though the individual is very hungry and obsessively capable of steering away from food. A classic case might be the person passionately cooking food for others, but eating nothing themselves: it becomes a kind of display of strength. All this seems to relate to the idea of the homunculus.

We need to exclude some other serious disorders before making a diagnosis about anorexia. Weight loss can be primary or secondary, and other possible causes have to be eliminated first. An exact diagnosis therefore revolves around basic headings, which might refer to any psychological abnormality that could be described as weight phobia. In females, for example, there are obvious symptoms to be considered, such as response to low temperature, being dehydrated, having a slow heart rate or increased hair on the face and body, as well as many other blood tests, the results of which may be way below the normal.

Some studies of twins have shown that two people with the same genetic framework can respond in very different ways. At this stage in Western society, on the whole women want to be slimmer and men usually want to be heavier, but selectively so; muscle not fat. There has been a marked increase in weight and height for the under-30 population. Excess pressure from the ideal of slimness embodied in ballerinas, athletes and models, who are not only admired for their shape but also their control, is an important factor in the obsessive way in which weight control is sometimes managed by teenagers. There are family issues to be considered, too, such as the extent to which the individual has been encouraged to take control and deal with everyday problems. In some cases, the loss of a parent either through death or divorce may be an important factor.

Back to the homunculus. We know what we look like from the outside when we stand in front of the mirror, but from the inside our brain's interpretations might be totally different. This includes movement, sensation and appearance, all interacting to create our self-image. There are studies in normal individuals that indicate that, in both sexes, by and large we both over- and underestimate such things as arm and leg length, shoulder width and ordinary features.

We know that both the sensory and motor parts of the brain above the ear have larger parts of this homunculus. Genetically, this affects how we operate on a day-to-day basis and the way we use our bodies. As an example, tennis players will imagine they have, as well as actually possess, larger arms and forearms: they will exist as an image in the appropriate sensory cortex. The underlying point here is that with eating disorders all of this is greatly exaggerated and distorted, with probably anorexia nervosa most of all; visualizing the stomach to be very much bigger than it is in reality.

These disorders seem to cover virtually every aspect of day-to-day life within the family. In addition, the causes seem complex – a confection of a great many factors which vary widely from individual to individual, or at different times even within the same person. The situation is made more complicated when one considers the impact of depression. Depression is also difficult to assess, but certainly around half of young people diagnosed seem to have features relating to both that and anxiety, with social phobias and obsessive-compulsiveness important elements.

Tony: Let's try and pull this together. What should parents be looking for, and how should they go about dealing with it?

Herb: In most cases we're talking about girls, but this is about boys as well. Characteristically, there is a good deal of self-hatred and isolation: downy hair over the arms and parts of the body, swathing themselves in thick clothing because they feel cold; keeping very active but still feeling fat and grotesque; fascinated with food but only for others (therefore appearing very busy in the kitchen). There is a dramatic and rather obvious weight loss, a habit of making comments about feeling fat, especially in certain parts of the body, constant attention to the weighing scales, regular use of laxatives or purgatives, making excuses to stay away from the table. Cessation of periods may be an issue with girls, too. Also, as so many young women use oral contraceptives, the normal usual symptom of amenorrhoea is no longer applicable.

Tony: We know it's highly likely a teenager will refuse to admit there's a problem, let alone draw attention to it. We know too that there's professional help available, but how can parents bridge the gap? What do you do with your obstructive and reluctant teenage child when you are convinced there might be an eating disorder?

Herb: A real-life story may be the best way to answer that question. I remember seeing a 16-year-old girl who was a very popular sportswoman, successful at school and fully part of a loving family. This changed very dramatically when a boy at school, probably as a ham-fisted compliment, used the unfortunate phrase 'thunder thighs', which she took to be an appalling criticism of her shape. Almost all the dramatic symptomatology described above was an immediate consequence. It did, however, take more than a year before family, the school, the GP and others were able to persuade her to seek treatment as an alternative to hospitalization. This was a fairly long process, involving both family therapy and cognitive behavioural therapy, to which she responded reasonably well. It took rather longer before she settled down more convincingly, and the advent of an admiring boyfriend when she was 19 was the turning point. This, unfortunately, is not easy to prescribe!

Tony: As I have seen time and again, the problem for many parents, particularly those who are used to quick decisions and outcomes in their professional lives, is that there is no quick fix. Parents need considerable patience, and there are no shortcuts. It can, understandably enough, be very frustrating. The key thing is that parents mustn't give up.

BINGE EATING

Tony: Anorexia nervosa is the most common eating disorder, and is certainly the condition I have come across most frequently in school, but what other similar conditions, like bulimia, have come your way?

Herb: Bulimia is frequently coupled with anorexia, but is a different condition involving regular bouts of binge-eating followed by self-induced vomiting. Bulimics eat substantial portions of food within a couple of hours, having no control, and as a result they vomit. They often misuse laxatives or diuretics, fast between sessions or exercise excessively. There are huge overlaps between anorexia nervosa and bulimia in symptomatology, but this does not have any real influence on the way in which the conditions should be treated.

Binge-eating disorder (BED) is basically a condition in which self-induced vomiting occurs after far larger quantities of food than normal are ingested over a two-hour period. Eating is associated with loss of control, more often than not in isolation, with eating very quickly and when not even hungry. There are clear overlaps with bulimia. In a nutshell, BED is too quick, too full, too much, too embarrassing and depressing, at least once a week over three months.

Conditions like these are often associated with other diagnoses such as anxiety disorders and obsessive-compulsive disorder, or even depression, but it goes even further than that. A small percentage might have a co-morbid autism spectrum disorder. All in all, this is serious stuff requiring rapid intervention, with as much outpatient therapeutic work as possible in an attempt to avoid admission to hospital.

Tony: In some cases I have seen significant, even dramatic, medical side-effects which were unexpected. What are these?

Herb: There is a whole range of possible medical ramifications, including slow heart rate and low blood pressure, muscle loss and weakness, severe dehydration and possible kidney disease, reduction of bone density, swelling of ankles and other parts of the body, damage to heart muscles and possible heart failure. Then there is anaemia, constipation, lanugo hair (the body's attempt to keep it warm), arrested growth and so on. All of this in addition to obvious dry skin and hair and nails, together with depression and even suicidal mood swings. The whole body is under threat.

The recommended therapeutic work for all of these includes family-based therapy (FBT), cognitive behavioural therapy (CBT), group work for families and similar affected individuals, and also adolescent-focused therapy (AFT). Each case is different, which is why good professional help at the earliest stage is so important.

BODY SHAPE

Tony: We have talked about body image in the context of anorexia and bulimia, but it's still an issue even when the symptoms of these conditions are not quite so apparent. All adolescents go through a highly self-conscious phase in which they become acutely aware of their own bodies, particularly by comparison with others. Inevitably, other people look better. This is part of the human condition. Robbie Burns was pretty near the mark when he wrote, 'Oh, would some power the giftie gie us, to see ourselves as others see us.' What's to be said about the great mass of young people as they work their way through this uncomfortable, sometimes distressing, but natural process? I suppose you are now going to tell me that this is a defined condition?

Herb: There is indeed: body dysmorphic disorder (BDD). The condition is extremely common in young adults and teenagers of both sexes: well over 90 per cent in both, with girls more affected than boys are. Almost invariably, there are more issues involved in the disorder than just appearance and weight. Far too many young people have a tendency to continue with these negative feelings in later life. In the vast majority of young people almost all of this revolves around perceptions of body shape and size, with what they see as ideal images on screen, in magazines and so on (with many of these images Photoshopped). As a result, virtually impossible targets are self-imposed, with what adolescents see as failure being the outcome and anxiety and depression the consequence. Spain, France and Ireland took a stand recently by banning the use of super-thin models in advertising. I would make advertising of this kind illegal in all countries.

Tony: There are plenty of vested interests to resist such a move. While the online world can seem dominant, it can produce some interesting counter-reactions. I'm aware of teenagers who become very focused on what they perceive to be healthy eating. On the one hand, this can be rather refreshing, a kind of antidote to thinness culture, but it can become obsessional in itself. There's a kind of virtuous self-righteousness that permeates their thinking.

Herb: Taken to extreme this is part of a condition I have already described: *orthorexia*. This is when individuals are critically bewildered about how others can eat so badly. They feel totally in control of what is seen as the correct diet; they are virtuous because they only consume 'good foods'. They feel great pleasure when complimented on their appearance, which they attribute solely to the eating pattern they have adopted. I would place it somewhere between avoidant restrictive food intake disorder and anorexia nervosa, and it is often misdiagnosed as the latter. It's related to fads and diets.

SOME THOUGHTS ON DIETS AND FADS

Tony: Vegetarianism has a long and rather noble history in the West. Over the past 100 years there has been a growing number of people who purport to feel better both physically and morally as a consequence of their decision not to eat meat or fish. Veganism is a more recent phenomenon.

Even so, the Vegan Society in Britain estimates that there are over half a million adherents in this country. There are twice as many women as men, and many of them choose to be lifestyle vegans, who avoid products tested on animals and wear clothes free from animal products such as leather, wool, silk and the like. As so often, celebrity endorsement and social media have accelerated the cause. There are said to be more than 61 million posts listed on Instagram about veganism. Flexitarianism (part-time vegans or vegetarians) is on the rise, too. These are well-intentioned and thoughtful people: my grandfather took to print as a passionate advocate of vegetarianism in the 1930s. This seems all to the good – but you have some doubts.

Herb: It's difficult for medical people to understand, because of our evolutionary past and the way in which we have been designed. We have specific teeth and enzymes created for us to be omnivores: that is to say, we are able and willing to eat virtually everything. Some societies value grubs and insects and other very strange foodstuffs which we would find abhorrent, but we are all internally exactly the same under the skin. The differences, therefore, arise between the ears, in other words the way we think and feel. As a result, cutting out groups of food and dieting very seriously means an inevitable series of deficiencies in our day-to-day functioning.

Tony: I have seen top-level, successful schoolboy sportsmen thrive as vegetarians. Are they an anomaly, or are you making too much of the issue?

Herb: Whether we like it or not, we need proteins of all sorts, carbohydrates, vitamins, high-fibre, trace elements and possibly other things we have yet to discover. If we cut back on calories to a considerable extent, the body has a need to store more – usually fat, which is hardly the intention! In addition, hunger is often present, and interferes with other mental functioning and activities. It may well be that the rise in veganism is in some way a response to the levels of obesity seen elsewhere, not just a moral objection. My point is that the full implications for health have yet to be evaluated, on not just a physical, but also an emotional level. It's usually not health reasons that lead to a belief in dietary exclusions, but the emotional turmoil of having to kill and cook living organisms.

Tony: So from a medical point-of-view, you're advising caution about any dietary exclusion. Don't exclude a food unless there is a proven, good cause to do so. What about exclusions which are advertised as being health-enhancing – gluten, for example?

Herb: For a start, all gluten-free foodstuffs are at least double or even four times the price of normal foods: they are also less nutritious and more fattening. They tend to be tasteless, so have to be bolstered by increased fat sugar and other additives.

Tony: This kind of diet is now very popular in the West. One only has to look at a typical newspaper or television programme and see the number of celebrities involved to appreciate how much press coverage this generates. People feel they are taking some kind of control by actively scrutinizing their diet and eliminating potentially harmful substances. This is understandable, so what's wrong?

Herb: Yes, but only 1 per cent of the population suffers from Coeliac disease, which is an autoimmune disorder. This means that there is a reaction from eating gluten, which is a protein found in barley rye and wheat, etc. The reaction takes place in the small bowel and can cause a number of distressing symptoms even in fairly young children, including weight loss, fatigue, diarrhoea, constipation and vomiting and distinctly pale, foul stools. In adults, it can develop at virtually any age as a response to multiple factors, such as a viral disease, surgery and even emotional stress. There is said to be a genetic predisposition to the disorder which can therefore be triggered at any stage of life. It can be diagnosed by blood test, or if necessary by an examination of the small bowel. Coeliac disease is a serious matter; however, two-thirds or more of those sticking to a gluten-free diet do not suffer from it.

Tony: I can still see that removing something potentially harmful from their diet would give anyone the impression that they would therefore be fitter and healthier.

Herb: But there are definite health risks in a self-imposed diet of this kind which isn't necessary. There is an increased incidence of obesity because of the decrease in fibre intake, which is known to prevent the development of diabetes: gluten-free might be a quick pathway to that disorder amongst other things. Low-fibre intake increases the risk of colon cancer and heart disease, and many crucial vitamins and nutrients are not available for absorption. There are very high levels of heavy metals in the blood of those on gluten-free diets: mercury, lead, arsenic and so on, possibly due to an excessive intake of seafood and rice in order to avoid gluten. The message is simple: go gluten-free only if you have a genuine medical condition.

Tony: Crohn's disease is a related condition that adolescents can face.

Herb: Yes, it is a rather more serious condition, autoimmune as well, but triggering inflammation throughout the bowel, as well as eyes and joints on occasion.

Avoiding gluten might be helpful, but many sufferers of Crohn's disease have no problem with the grains we have mentioned. Crohn's might need medical or even surgical treatment because of the pain and discomfort.

OBESITY

Herb: As a medical student I was intrigued to read that some 300 years ago Benjamin Franklin had a sign in his office which read: 'I saw few men die of hunger; of eating, one hundred thousand!' That's certainly going back some considerable time, but it illustrates the fact that being too fat is not just a modern problem. Obesity is increasing in Westernised societies and is a considerable risk factor for any of the eating disorders, let alone Type 2 diabetes, which is a serious and potentially fatal condition. Other important health issues include heart disease, strokes and even some kinds of cancers.

Tony: Popular press coverage attributes this increase in obesity to sofa-surfing, obsession with screens generally, together with fast foods and a lack of physical exercise. On the other hand, some people, particularly those who are overweight, point to genetics as the unconquerable cause. What's the truth of it?

Herb: Genetics is part of the problem, but nowhere near as much some people like to think. Several studies have related genetic predisposition for obesity to many genetic variants in both males and females, and have come to the conclusion that healthy diet is the most important way of remaining fit and well. A recent American study, perhaps a little unkindly, shows that genetics are no excuse for a weak response to personal practice and health policy. This applies both to individuals and governments attempting to tackle the problem. The yardstick that is used is body-mass index (BMI). This is arrived at by measuring height and weight according to gender and age, and specific charts are available on the web both for professionals and anyone who wants to look it up. A BMI of 30 or over is regarded as obese, and one between 18 and 25 is seen as healthy.

Tony: I assume the way to look at this is that our choice of diet, particularly fatty, fried foods and excessive sugar consumption, magnifies the influence of genetics on the way in which we gain weight.

Herb: Yes, bearing in mind that two-thirds of what makes us fat comes from diet, and only about 20 per cent can be regarded as hereditary. This is not really good news for those people who claim obesity is simply a family-based problem and cannot be helped. There are some new, interesting studies on gut bacteria (microbiome), suggesting that altering these is an approach for the future which might be a valuable way of tackling intractable obesity. It would seem that fat storage in the body is influenced by the food and drink we consume. For the moment, however, that methodology has yet to be firmly established, which means that dieting still remains the gold standard for losing weight.

Tony: Dangerous levels of obesity in young people are said to have reached crisis proportions. More than a third of the children who leave primary school are recorded as being overweight. Of these, over 4 per cent are seriously obese. This is a very different picture from the period just after the Second World War, when poor children were on average 2kg lighter than their rich counterparts. This is now reversed. Why should this be so?

Herb: Let's face it, it's easier to feed a family with so-called junk food, and cheaper, too. This includes burgers, chicken nuggets, prepared supermarket meals, frozen foods, cheap pizzas and so on. To buy fresh fruit and vegetables, fish and meat and prepare all of this at home is more expensive and not necessarily an enjoyable exercise. Fresh food also has an unpleasant tendency to go off rapidly.

Tony: In the UK considerable sums of money are being spent on producing healthy school meals, trying to arrange for more exercise for the young and providing a constant drip feed of advice to parents and young people themselves, yet there has been no real breakthrough. Twenty-five per cent of boys in the UK at age 11 are regarded as obese. This is a problem in most Western countries: the equivalent number affected in Greece and Malta is around 33 per cent and, at the lower end, Denmark and the Netherlands are at around 13 per cent. Despite the range in statistics, it's clear there is a shared, underlying problem.

Herb: Part of the problem has been encouraging so-called healthy choices by providing the wrong information. This has come both from the food industry and the pharmaceutical companies, and has been an exercise in futility. Even government advice has not always been as accurate as it might be. Remember the cholesterol and saturated fats story, the danger of eating eggs and all those desirable low-fat preparations which contained large quantities of sugar. Yet such is our failure to take personal responsibility that many now believe the state must take over: that the failure of society and education has obliged the nanny state to intervene. Sugar taxes, greater attention to prepared food contents, relocation of fast food outlets, limiting junk-food price promotions, restricting sponsorship of youth activities by brands linked to poor nutritional products, advice to retailers about what should be removed from checkout areas: all are now under the microscope.

Tony: This is a case where state and family must share responsibility equally. It's clearly an issue for government, not least because there are overwhelming cost implications for the NHS, which will need to deal with the medical consequences of the rise in obesity, but families must be engaged in the solution. As so often, it's a question of educating not just children but all of us in adult society too, particularly parents. We can't underestimate the scorn and stigma often directed at obese teenagers, which can be very harmful to their all-round development. How do we help people to lose weight so they feel comfortable socially, physically and psychologically?

Herb: In the first place, I would issue a caution about drugs. There are many drugs on the market which claim to decrease appetite, and some of them do, but all of them have undesirable side-effects, including the tendency to be habit-forming. Gastric band surgery is undoubtedly effective in shrinking the ability of the stomach to deal with fluid intake, but is unlikely to be available for everyone, even if they wanted to have it. Biologically, losing weight is a complicated business. For example, the hormone ghrelin increases appetite and weight, is produced by the stomach and is fast-acting; by contrast, leptin is derived from fat cells and decreases appetite, but is quite slow-acting in terms of possible weight loss. Paradoxically, obese people have an increase of leptin in their systems, but appear to be resistant to its effects, so hunger cravings do not stop as they should.

Tony: Which suggests to me that if someone is serious about losing weight, there is no escape from old-fashioned methods which take some determination and time to take effect. A healthy diet and exercise.

Herb: There is certainly now evidence to suggest that old-fashioned ways work. For example, a ten-year Canadian study tracked hundreds of children from the age of five months to ten years. The results show conclusively that those who had regular meals with the family were much healthier than their counterparts who did not. There were benefits socially and psychologically, but also the measured intake of food and drink had a positive impact on possible obesity outcomes

Tony: That's fine, but the ideal of the family meal has probably slipped too far into the past to be relevant to many modern families. There's a fascinating contrast with the French, geographically so close, but much further away from the UK in terms of food culture. Family meals are more common, the choice of food in a school is greater, and there is not the same condoned habit of snacking; vending machines and smartphones are banned in school, so playtimes are for physical exercise, not gaming, texting and eating. The French are pretty blunt about obesity, too – *grossophobie*, a kind of public shaming, seems not just permissible but even encouraged. We may not want to go all the way down this route, but the evidence shows that obesity in French children is at significantly lower levels than in the UK or US.

Herb: Maybe it's because they smoke so much! There's also an issue about the time of day we eat. Another study has shown that the later one eats at night, the more likely one is to have increased cholesterol and insulin levels, with an overall negative effect on fat metabolism.

Tony: Eat late, gain weight! It's interesting that some Asian countries with a reputation for healthy eating tend to have an evening meal around 6 p.m. Families will make their own arrangements, but it seems pretty clear that each family should agree some plan which includes a regular timetable, so that teenagers, in particular, don't just drift into a habit of grazing on unhealthy foods late into the night.

Herb: The other dimension is exercise. The NHS, among others, offers good, practical advice and support about increased physical activity. Often this advice is about simple things, such as walking rather than using the car or public transport, taking the stairs rather than the lift, and making more of an effort to change entrenched lifestyles. Comparisons are sometimes drawn with campaigns to stop smoking, which in many respects have been remarkably successful. While increasing the price of food is not a practical option (unlike cigarettes), banning advertisements of unhealthy food, insisting on unattractive, informative packaging and encouraging social disapproval might all usefully play their part in changing the climate.

Tony: The nub of it seems to be *Understand – Eat healthily – Exercise*. And take responsibility for yourself and your family.

AVOIDING BEING HANGRY

Herb: I've just come across the term *hangry*. This is an amalgam of the words hungry and angry, and has now entered the *Oxford English Dictionary*. Scientists have confirmed that hunger can lead to irritability and acting out; this is not simply due to a decrease in blood sugar levels as we used to think. It's probably a complicated emotional response to our personalities, personal biology and the cues in our environment at the time.

Tony: That's a good way to conclude this chapter! Avoiding being hangry should be a good target for us all, just as much as avoiding obesity or obsessions with food. Parents and teachers can be central in creating the environment in which adolescents are encouraged to be honest with themselves about eating habits, and to think things through.

7

Emotional Turbulence

Tony: This is probably one of the most difficult areas for us to discuss, not least because everyone experiences some kind of emotional turbulence along the way. It's certainly a challenge for schools. Emotional life has greater prominence in the way teachers think and schools operate than used to be the case. When I started, the emotional well-being of children was largely seen to be their own business, but it was clear to me from the outset that the most respected teachers had an intuitive understanding of teenagers' emotional needs and supported them. Inevitably, with greater openness comes a greater awareness of the sheer range of emotional issues that young people face.

Herb: The causes of emotional difficulty are varied and overlap, including heredity, family function, stress and how it is dealt with, even diet. One or more of these can lead to difficulties which are perfectly normal, but can become all-encompassing and dangerous, with extremes of despair and thinking about suicide.

Tony: It's worth pointing out the obvious, which is sometimes underplayed: mental problems occur at any age in every society, every religion, in every race, and in all classes from the very rich to the very poor, from the very well-nourished to the starving, from the overindulged to the totally neglected. This is part of the human condition experienced by everybody at some stage or another, to a greater or lesser degree.

Herb: The point is that most disturbances will resolve themselves but, if not, can be treated, and should not be regarded as arising from an inherent personal weakness or social circumstance.

Tony: Let's start by focusing on the prerequisites for good emotional health.

Herb: A handful of basics, easily described, but not necessarily always attainable, or sustainable:

1 Being physically fit and well.
2 Feeling fully supported in key areas of life, which includes family, school, and friends; religious identity comes into this to a considerable extent for some.
3 Having interests, both physical and intellectual, and maintaining and developing them regularly.
4 Being able to belong to social clubs and other activities outside school, and continuing to do so at university or training or having started a job.
5 Maintaining balance, without concentrating on one or more to the detriment of other elements of healthy normality.

Tony: We know that ups and downs are normal and should be recognized as such, but I've seen situations when these normal low moods become medicalized, which seems to be superimposing a new problem. Is your profession at fault? Are you making things worse?

Herb: There's some truth in that. For example, it's highly likely that too many university students are referred for psychological treatment because they have mood swings or feel depressed, when the actual cause is excessive or unreachable work targets or loneliness, rejection by a close companion or simply missing home. A little reluctantly, I have to concede that too many GPs under pressure of work find it easier to dish out unnecessary sick notes, thus increasing absenteeism. That said, perhaps the worst phrase in the English language is 'Pull yourself together.' As in most things, there's a balance. Getting it right is easy to talk about but difficult to put into practice, even for experienced professionals.

Tony: Some reports suggest there has been a fivefold increase over the past decade in young people reporting mental health issues during their first year at university. Part of this might be simply be adjusting to a new rhythm, especially if it's the first time away from home.

Herb: Loneliness, in particular, is too often misdiagnosed as being depression. We are the first country in the world, it would seem, that actually possesses a Minister for Loneliness. She has reported that it's most likely in 16- to 24-year-olds, although the elderly constitute a large number as well. Government recognition of mental health issues is a remarkable and promising step in the right direction, not least for financial reasons.

Tony: I've seen figures that suggest something like ten million people in the UK suffer from the effects of loneliness. ChildLine has recently reported a 14 per cent rise in the number of children who contacted them about loneliness problems, mostly young girls. Feeling lonely can be brief and recurring, but can become a long-term disability.

Herb: If there are genuine problems such as illness or death and there's no one to share difficulties with, loneliness becomes accentuated, with very few stimuli to prevent or divert thoughts that lead to misery. There's then a direct connection between mental and physical illness. The internet can provide bad advice.

Tony: Common sense suggests that having friends to confide in and engaging in activities on a regular basis, such as sport or the performing arts, are among the most effective ways to deal with loneliness. Is that supported by the available research?

Herb: Yes. University counselling services, such as they are, might be helping, or achieving nothing, or causing harm. The President of the Royal Society of Medicine, Sir Simon Wessely, has recently stated that universities are over-medicalizing the normal emotions of young adults, thereby fuelling a need to increase responses to perceived mental health difficulties. This is an unnecessary expense, and might be making matters worse. Nevertheless, that doesn't mean there are sufficient resources available in such a stressful environment.

Tony: The issue, then, is what's put in place to encourage students to connect in the way you've described. Good schools have systems of pastoral care that embrace everyone, but this is not so at all universities: they could learn a great deal from the way good schools operate. Offering medical support when things have gone wrong, but offering very little in the way of pastoral care, is just not logical.

Herb: Not all schools can provide it. Recent figures (2018) from NHS England reveal that almost 400,000 children and young people are receiving treatment for mental health problems. The vast majority are in the under-19 age group, and the number has risen by a third over the last two years. The main areas are depression, anxiety and eating disorders.

Tony: There are plenty of people out there, like the charity Young Minds, who would agree with you that there is insufficient help. They talk about a new conflagration. What one might call the 'traditional' causes are still there, including family dynamics and pressure at school, but it's the overwhelming influence of social media that appears to have fuelled mental health issues.

Herb: This is exacerbated because many GPs are reluctant to refer young people, even though they acknowledge the need for help, as they believe the extraordinarily long waiting times at CAMHS (Child and Adolescent Mental Health Services) and other agencies make it a pointless exercise. Somewhat astonishingly, NHS England concedes that only a quarter of under-18s with an identified mental health problem have treatment made available to them. It hopes that will increase to over a third in two or more years! The problems are many, not least that recruitment of child and adolescent psychiatrists has been falling, and finding beds for young people is like gold dust – all this at a time when there are more mental health referrals than ever before. There are frequent reports of acutely suicidal young people placed on long waiting lists or referred for treatment at centres far away from where they live. In most cases, some form of family-based therapy is essential for a good outcome. This isn't possible if treatment is miles away.

ANXIETY DISORDERS

Tony: Faced with the sheer volume of problems, it would be too easy to retreat and respond with a collective shrug of the shoulders. Yet all of us in a family or in a school have the ability to help directly. Better understanding and knowledge provide the confidence to feel able to do so.

Herb: I agree. The initial problem should be dealt with either by self-diagnosis or by family, teachers or friends, and only then referred onwards if the situation is not resolved. Anxiety disorders are the most common psychological disorders in the Western world, with a lifetime prevalence of almost 30 per cent. The commonest is social anxiety disorder, often described as social phobia, and it can start in very early adolescence. By late adolescence it will be extremely prominent in a large percentage.

Tony: I've seen this phobia frequently in schools. I remember one large, confident-looking boy arriving at the age of 16 as a boarder for the first time. He spent most of the first six months on the verge of tears, and it was a real effort of will for him to return to school after each break. By the time he left school at the age of 18, he was fully adjusted, successful and on his way to a top university. More to the point, he was delighted that he had stuck it out. That he had been able to do so was due partly to his own resilience, but also to the sustained, supportive attention of boarding-house staff, parents and his peers.

Herb: Freud accurately described anxiety as 'the common coin of emotion'. There are some 80 varieties of presentations of various illnesses in which anxiety and depression can be prominent features. These include: alcoholism, asthma, caffeine-related psychiatric disorders, various drug overdoses, personality disorders, primary insomnia, Lyme disease and even Type I Diabetes Mellitus. Diagnosing an anxiety-type disorder requires a full and careful medical history, not least to exclude the many illnesses which can present initially in a very dramatic fashion, sidelining the real cause of the problem.

Tony: Many books and articles have been published about anxiety, and it's a subject that continues to be researched and expanded upon. It's a crowded field of literature. Despite all this information, one area that seems to be unclear is the distinction between anxiety and fear.

Herb: Fear is the sensation of alarm and response to some perceived danger, while anxiety, which exhibits similar bodily sensations, may not relate to anything readily identifiable. The adrenaline response of fight or flight (or freeze) is an important survival technique in all animals, and includes physical and biochemical changes in the body as well as extreme psychological ones. These reactions are particular to an individual: we do not experience the same situation the same way and respond accordingly. It's this subjectivity which differentiates so much of what we feel and react to as individuals rather than as a group. We're used to seeing herd instinct demonstrated in natural history documentaries on television – animals taking flight together or grouping together in response to an attack. Humans may respond in that way, or may not. We are complicated creatures.

Tony: Fear is not always an unpleasant thing, though. We go to a horror movie or a classical tragedy in part to be frightened, or at least have our fear exorcized. So it provides excitement and can be very addictive. It's what drives young men in particular into some very risky behaviour.

Herb: Endorphins are among the other drivers. These morphine-like substances, produced in response to strenuous physical activity, may or may not be dangerous and/or pleasurable. Adrenaline and noradrenaline play an important role in biochemical changes which give us the pleasurable sensations so actively sought after. It's not only strenuous physical activity which gives this desirable response: it also presents in gambling, shoplifting, speeding well beyond the limit, watching dangerous sporting activity and, essentially, all pleasurable fear-promoting activities (see Chapter 8, Happiness Hormones).

Tony: Even the apparently less dangerous responses to endorphins can be worrying. Addictive exercise, for example, is much healthier than gambling or shoplifting, but it causes its own problems. Teenagers can become addicted to performance-enhancement supplements for bodybuilding. The quest for the body beautiful, whether for a boy or a girl, can be an addiction in itself, and makes them vulnerable to the promise of advertisements: eat this, drink that, look like this.

Herb: Some endorphins can be seen to have a broader social good: standing up to bullies, being brave enough to disagree with an authority figure; excelling at contact sports.

Tony: I'm glad you raised that point. It seems to me that some degree of stress and anxiety is crucial: it increases achievement and stimulates our learning and our psychological development; without it, nothing much happens and we settle into a comfortably safe inertia. I have sometimes wished school students would exhibit a little *more* anxiety and stress. I once had a serious discussion with senior colleagues about the help that was needed to calm down stressed girls before public exams, leading to a debate about a seemingly relaxed group of boys of the same age who were being supercool and laid back in response!

Herb: There's a difference between trait anxiety and state anxiety: the former is a permanent chronic feature of a personality, the latter a temporary phenomenon occurring in specific situations such as examinations and, it's hoped, keeping the brain at peak performance levels for the short periods of time required. Trait anxiety is altogether less desirable, both for the individuals and those around them.

Tony: So we should see most forms of stress as being potentially beneficial – up to a point. It's when the thrill of achievement proves short-lived and needs repetition in order to be satisfying that we enter dangerous territory. As a parent, teacher or friend we shouldn't see the endorphin as a foe to our teenager, but we should take note when symptoms reach an intensity and frequency that are worrying.

Herb: Yes, and early help is infinitely preferable to waiting until it has become uncontrollable. As in so much, open talk early on can give huge benefits.

Tony: Particularly when it comes from friends. A child's anxiety can be very tough for parents to deal with. I've had some very concerned that their five- or six-year-old child has developed what seems a profound school phobia.

Herb: This is a difficult area, because once failure to perform in an academic situation has arisen, often at a very early age, there is great resistance to change. This is the point at which the headings we discussed in Chapter 3 become significant. They are all interrelated and overlap to various degrees and at various times.

Tony: The role of parents in reinforcing a child's timidity is well-established: the fledgling not pushed out of the nest never learns to fly properly. Velcro parenting (overprotection, over-concern, doing for the child what the child should be doing) is hardly adequate preparation for future independence. This is part of a bigger picture around the world: I have no doubt that more and more parents seem to feel the need to live their children's lives for them, a kind of vicarious pleasure and self-validation. Ambition, support and drive are one thing, but the obsession of the results-driven Tiger mum (or dad) is very damaging to children. A variation on the theme is the Helicopter parent, not so single-minded as the Velcro type, but someone who perpetually hovers and casts a shadow over the child.

Herb: Parents need to be able to step back and see themselves as working quietly behind the scenes. They need to prompt, even push their child into positive self-functioning territory. Appropriate praise and obvious pleasure in response to achievements keep good personality development on track. Anger, hostility, indifference and competitiveness are destructive.

Tony: This is particularly the case when parents express rage or anger over bad examination results or an uncomfortable school report. Parental frustration might cause their child to stop and think, but the frustration itself gets nowhere. Often the young person feels (perhaps misguidedly) that they have actually been working reasonably well.

Herb: We know that young people see themselves as moving on a single linear course, and their perceptions about the future and their lives in general will derive from the way the past has unfolded. So much depends on the way in which parents have spoken about and managed the successes and potential failures of their children. Inevitably, young people will identify very strongly with parents, either positively or negatively. Feeling assisted and supported helps personality development, but constant criticism and denigration have the opposite effect.

Tony: It comes down to parents being good role models. Learning by example continues throughout early development and well into adolescence. A calm and supportive adult authority figure is the bedrock.

SPECIFIC ANXIETY DISORDERS

Herb: There are some specific anxiety disorders which particularly affect teenagers. There's a cultural context to different presentations of anxiety, an example being that panic disorder ranges from nearly 3 per cent in Italy to less than half a per cent in Taiwan. In America there is no apparent difference in the rates of panic disorder among various races; however, the male-to-female ratio of lifetime anxiety disorders is 2:3. Interestingly, in some Far Eastern cultures social anxiety disorders relate to worries about being offensive to other people rather than being embarrassed about oneself.

Tony: That's been my experience in China. Worldwide, most social phobias begin well before late adolescence, with age 16 being the median, but, as I understand it, panic disorders can kick in at any time.

Herb: Yes, they can start from mid-adolescence and also in midlife. Obsessive-compulsive disorders tend to begin from late adolescence onwards. The simple phobias, such as fear of spiders or any other commonly seen object, develop fairly early on and usually disappear. Simple or specific phobias as well as social phobias tend to be primary: that is to say, they don't need a trigger to cause them. On the other hand, agoraphobia, a fear of going out in public and open spaces, tends to be a secondary phenomenon. It's long-standing, whereas panic attacks with sudden onset may look like agoraphobia. All very worrying to them and all around them.

There are two international classification manuals in common use: the American Psychiatric Association's DSM–5 and the ICD 11 (the International Classification of Diseases), used by the World Health Organisation. The Diagnostic and Statistical Manual of Mental Disorders (DSM–5) is probably the most useful. Using the conditions listed in the DSM–5 as the starting point, the main disorders with which families have to deal are:

General Anxiety Disorder (GAD) – occurs when the sufferer worries about everyday events, however innocuous they might seem.

Agoraphobia – occurs when a person perceives their environment to be unsafe, with no easy way to get out (which includes open spaces, public transport, shopping centres or just being outside the home). This can lead to extremes of avoidance behaviour and make functioning at school virtually impossible.

Separation Anxiety Disorder – occurs when the pain of separation is felt so strongly that it becomes a specific psychiatric diagnosis (common in children, but can also occur in older adolescents and adults).

Acute Stress Disorder – occurs when exposure to any traumatic event (accidents, death, disaster, etc.) leads to severe anxiety within a month, characterized by altered perceptions of reality, difficulty in experiencing positive emotions and inability to remember the event.

PTSD Post-Traumatic Stress Disorder – occurs when experiencing or witnessing anything which leads to extreme fear, possibly of dying oneself, or any life-threatening and frightening situation. Triggers can include a short episode of violence, abuse of any kind including sexual, and witnessing or being part of a serious accident. Symptoms do not necessarily begin immediately, and may occur very much later, often measured in years. This is an important diagnosis in all age groups.

Panic attacks, including claustrophobia are stressful and very common. The symptoms of a classic panic attack are hyperventilation, rapid heart rate with dizziness, disorientation, dry mouth, chest pain, breathing difficulties, confusion, sweating, etc. An example is claustrophobia, when an irrational and terrifying fear of being closed in without escape leads to a panic attack. Sufferers go to extraordinary lengths to avoid triggers. As an example of the irrationality of it all, some people believe that tight clothing, especially around the neck, can elicit exactly the same sort of attack. A typical incident was witnessing a passenger stuck in a long, slow-moving queue at immigration becoming flushed and vexed, then falling into a screaming fit and having to be rescued and removed from the scene.

The best treatment is cognitive behavioural therapy (CBT), but antidepressants and drugs for anxiety have also been used, though these only offer temporary respite. Part of the treatment programme might include gradual desensitization, such as being accompanied by a therapist into a frightening area with relaxation and mindfulness exercises.

There are coping exercises that can work well. These include slow, deep breathing exercises with short pauses, constant self-reminders about the unreality of what is happening, remembering the previous attacks which passed without anything really appalling as an outcome, and taking a rest from any activity which seems to be leading to the problem, such as waiting on a crowded platform. A brief walk with breathing exercises could well curtail an impending attack.

Full descriptions of all these problems and other anxiety disorders can be found on websites such as those provided by the NHS and MIND.

DEPRESSION

Tony: It's probably impossible these days to discuss any age group without bringing in the vexed issue of depression. We know that depression occurs at all ages and stages of life. That these days celebrities and public figures are willing to talk about their problems in public has helped de-stigmatize a condition which almost everybody used to keep private from parents, professionals and even friends.

Herb: That's true, but we face great difficulty in diagnosing and dealing appropriately with such a potentially devastating condition. While in general terms there has been a decrease in teenage smoking, use of drugs and unwanted pregnancies, there's been a sharp increase in reported mental health issues, which is causing alarm in governments around the world.

Tony: 'Depression' is a colloquial term that can be used in a variety of ways, mostly to do with an understandable sadness with which we can identify and which requires little more than sympathy and general comforting. What we are concerned with here is something altogether more serious and deep-rooted.

Herb: The range of depressive moods runs from prolonged misery to really serious psychotic breakdown; different types of therapeutic approaches are needed depending on the circumstances. Professional help may well be needed. We should always be prepared to ask for advice, as unwillingness to do so can lead to extremely unhappy outcomes. The vast majority of sufferers will respond to simple lifestyle changes and specialist psychological approaches, such as Cognitive Behavioural Therapy.

Tony: There's a greater public awareness of the problems people face, but it's still the case that problems tend to be denied or brushed under the carpet. We live in a very competitive society. With teenagers and public exams, this competitiveness seems to override concerns about mental issues. It's as though by facing up to potential problems you forfeit your child's place in the Great Race. It's understandable that parents might judge their efficacy in terms of the achievements of their children, but to burden their children with the dead weight of expectation is one of the commonest causes of depressive illness in teenagers.

Herb: The triggers for depressive symptomatology are many and varied, but it's interesting that the worldwide situation (war, global warming, injustice) looms larger in the minds of young people than one might think; they are often acutely aware and concerned.

Tony: Other deep worries expressed to me have been about austerity, the constant change in modern society and a belief that the future is bleak.

Herb: And long waiting times for medical help. That said, personal, genuinely understandable circumstances with which anyone can identify are the most significant in depressive symptomatology.

Tony: Parents, naturally enough, are concerned about their child's happiness and performance in school. We make general assumptions, but there is a vicious circle: bad performance leads to depression and vice versa. Which tends to come first?

Herb: It's a revolving door: they feed on one another. Self-harm is associated with declining academic achievement, particularly at secondary school level; so, too, is substance abuse.

Tony: It seems that the whirlpool of depression surrounds each family, at least potentially so. Yet the diagnosis of clinical depression isn't easy, particularly if it's masked by other more evident and understandable factors in the individual concerned.

Herb: It's certainly the case that one half of those with eating disorders and most phobics, as well as one-third of those exhibiting conduct disorders, have an undercurrent of depression easily missed given the other factors.

Tony: Depression is a word used to cover any manner of feelings, but what is genuine, clinical depression?

Herb: The word is widely and wrongly used, but the DSM–5 definition includes: depressed mood, loss of pleasure and interest, decreased energy or aimless, restlessness, sleep or appetite disturbances, feelings of worthlessness, hopelessness or guilt for a period of at least two weeks, leading to significant distress and an inability to function. Other symptoms we notice, particularly with the young, are giving up activities about which they used to be enthusiastic, school refusal, feelings of shame (for whatever reason) and the need to feel secure and safe.

Tony: Sad to say, the end of school doesn't mean the end of depression. As we have noted, record numbers of university students are on waiting lists for counselling services, particularly women. These may well be adults according to the law, but they're often still young children in some respects. It isn't just a question of academic performance. In fact, that might be the least of their worries. Students always need to feel that they belong, so drinking, partying, late nights, missing lectures, while at the same time being concerned about fees, getting work done and having a plan for the future, are creating a potent cocktail.

Herb: On one level this seems difficult to understand. Millennials have a much better life than they believe is the case. Health is better, so is nutrition, there's more disposable income, but few see a positive future in which they might own their own homes and be free of debt. Some of this anxiety starts at an earlier age in the mid-teens, and the constant information overload means they are more informed than ever before, though not always accurately!

Tony: Which brings us neatly to the subject of smartphones. Wonderful in many ways though they are, they are also a dangerous infection. It's not so much headline aggression that sparks depression (being targeted by an internet troll is not an essential prerequisite to becoming depressed): far more significant is the shattering of self-image and self-esteem in an insidious way over time (see Chapter 9, Screenagers). As an interesting counterpoint, digital therapy is now being offered to 5- to 18-year-olds for mild depression – the internet being harnessed for mental health!

Herb: There is a sharp rise in the incidence of quite serious depressive disorders in young people, virtually double what it was ten years ago. Young people who spend far too much time on social media lag in general developmental terms. Although not the only reason for the marked increase in depressive symptomatology, it's often the case that the more depressed they are, the more likely they are to have spent excessive time on electronic devices.

Tony: What about treatments? At a time when reported mental illness is on the increase, there seem to be conflicting views, not least from your profession, about how best to help.

Herb: Let me approach this in a way you might not expect. A recent study that examined 120,000 people over 500 trials in 3 decades concluded somewhat emphatically that anti-depressants actually *do* work. This result was met with a degree of concern and even incredulity in some quarters, but I have never been in any doubt: the primary issue is which medication to use and to which patient it should be prescribed. Quite understandably, many young people and adults concerned for their welfare are highly resistant to the very idea of drugging as a form of treatment, but the alternative might simply be unthinkable. Nevertheless, there's always a danger that pills are given as a placebo, and it's hard to blame busy doctors with full surgeries for resorting to prescriptions. It's routinely claimed that over

10 per cent of British adults now take anti-depressants, but an Oxford study maintains that only one in six individuals who requires treatment is getting something appropriate. So, on the one hand medication has a bad name because of inappropriate prescribing but, on the other, those who scoffed at the very idea of anti-depressants are missing something potentially beneficial. One can't wholly subscribe to the view that big drug companies are pushing pills solely for profit, but research and development of wonder drugs needs funding or it stops.

Tony: Unlike other forms of medical treatment, it's hard for lay people to understand the concept of taking medication for mental illness, not least finding reliable, hard facts.

Herb: Well, the annual report of the Improving Access to Psychological Therapies Services (IAPT) notes that many people completing a full course of treatment have improved. Of the 1.4 million referred for this during 2016–17, almost half made a recovery. Full programmes revolve around talking therapies, to include cognitive behavioural therapy, interpersonal psychotherapy, counselling, mindfulness and other one-to-one or group interactions. Medication is important if appropriately prescribed. In terms of outcomes, it's interesting that there are ethnic group variations in recovery, with more than half of the white ethnic group recovering, rather less for others. Once again, I have to stress that it's another level of complexity if additional factors, like substance abuse, come into play.

Tony: You talk about the effectiveness of group and one-to-one therapies, but it seems that in the main adolescents are usually treated with medication and, even then, quite often a course of medication is not followed through.

There seems to be a considerable parental reaction against pretty much any form of treatment. Many are the times, sadly, I've met with parents who have spoken in a kind of code – not quite, 'A friend of mine has a problem,' but not far off it. One family refused to believe that medication would ever work, or that therapists had any validity whatsoever.

Herb: Several studies both in Europe and America have shown that even brief CBT provided by experts reduces depressive symptomatology to a considerable extent in young people. Although there's great support from government and others for confidential, trained counselling services being available in schools, too many have found the expense unsustainable. So there's a combination at work here: a negative parental reaction ('My child does not need pills/therapy'), and a limit on how far institutions and governments are prepared to fund treatments.

Tony: Parental wariness is understandable. Some might well feel, rightly or wrongly, that they're responsible for causing, or at least not preventing, the condition in their child. However, the most significant deterrent is a concern about confidentiality. Schools need to demonstrate that they are completely watertight around the counselling they offer. I've also sometimes questioned the motivation of a counsellor who seems to be gaining more from the experience than the patient! As a prospective parent for any school, I would now enquire about counselling provision. Are counsellors and therapists properly qualified and registered, and therefore bound by expectations of strict confidentiality? You can learn a lot about a school's culture when they talk about how they support young people with depression or other difficulties.

SUICIDE

Herb: There can surely be nothing more distressing for a family or anyone than to be associated with a suicide. This is particularly so when warning signals, like previous suicide attempts, have been ignored.

Tony: It's also extremely difficult for those acting *in loco parentis*. I have twice witnessed the effective end of the career of teachers directly responsible for suicide victims. They were both deeply affected, and neither could summon the ability to go on.

Herb: What's clear is that the situation is getting worse. Different countries have different ways of defining intent to die. Not surprisingly, in an attempt to avoid unnecessary hurt, an open verdict is often recorded. However, according to the NSPCC, the number of those receiving therapeutic sessions for suicidal thoughts rose from nearly 9,000 to over 22,000 between 2011 and 2017 – what a frightening and revealing figure!

Tony: As with a great deal of human behaviour, there are complex motives behind suicidal gestures: perhaps to draw attention to distress, or a suicide attempt may not actually have been intended at all, or at least not in full consideration of all the consequences: it may be an impulsive act as a result of a loss of self-esteem or anger, and it may be punitive ('My parents will be sorry when I'm gone').

Herb: It's probably best never to regard the suicidal gesture as a manipulative act, or even to suggest that it might be, given that the individual might subsequently feel the need to prove his or her point. This was brought home to me when I was a young medical student working in an A&E department of a large hospital. A 17-year-old boy was brought in as an emergency and died on the table. He had lived alone with his mother in a block of flats: whenever they had an argument he would put his head into the gas oven when she left home for work. He did this carefully, knowing exactly when she was due to return, and there had been previous, similar attempts, clearly with no intention on his part of dying. On this occasion, however, he saw his mother arriving when he looked out of the window, put his head in the oven, turned on the gas and waited. She stopped to talk to a neighbour and entered the flat 15 minutes later than usual: hence the outcome. It was an appalling business. This was back in the days of coal gas, but there are many other ways to cry for help without necessarily being manipulative. Neither he nor his mother had sought psychiatric help because of their shame and embarrassment.

Tony: Suicide and self-harm have been called 'the hidden epidemic', because so much never comes to the attention of professionals, or even individuals outside the family. Almost half of older adolescents report that at some point they've had suicidal thoughts, though without going any further. In a school context, actual acts of self-harm are invariably linked to stress, even anger, and are usually spontaneous, unplanned and dramatic. It strikes me that there's been a seasonal element to this, a touch of T. S. Eliot's 'April is the cruellest month.'

Herb: Most problems occur at nights and weekends: many people, the young in particular, are more depressed then because they perceive others are out and about doing desirable things. There is also an increase around Christmas and in springtime – indeed, April. Impulsivity is frequently the driver.

Tony: I've also been aware that secrecy and denial seem significant. I confess that I've never really been able to understand deliberate self-harming, like cutting, burning and severe scratching. It seems to be a public statement, yet mostly takes place in isolation, and the people who do it go to great lengths to cover up what they have done, wearing long trousers and long sleeves.

Herb: Yet many report great relief after cutting, however temporary this might be. Endorphin release is probably the cause. This is occasionally a group activity, more commonly with girls.

Tony: There seems to be a link between self-harming and overdosing, both of which are manifestations of emotional distress.

Herb: Yes, some do both. Overdosing usually occurs using substances such as paracetamol and other pharmacological medicaments easily obtainable. By a considerable margin this is the largest group referred for urgent hospital treatment, but it is very unusual to refer self-harmers: they are usually sent to out-patient psychiatric or psychological services – providing, of course, they can be found.

Tony: Over the years I've witnessed a variety of apparent motivations behind self-harm and suicide attempts. Genuine desire to die seems to me very rare; more often it really is the proverbial cry for help.

Herb: All cries for help should be taken seriously. Depression is high on the list of self-harmers. The list of causes includes family or school difficulties, girl/boyfriend problems, sexual identity confusions, drugs and alcohol, feeling physically ill and unable to cope. Persistent self-harm is potentially very serious, although few will actually commit suicide. It's important to check intent before doing anything else: what led them to this point; what they were thinking; what evidence there might be of advance planning; what were their expectations.

Tony: Copycat behaviour is a real concern in schools: the possibility of suicide can take a grip on the imaginations of teenagers. One school had four successful suicide attempts over a period of 18 months. The pressure on everyone in that community became intense. The headmaster admitted he felt helpless. In retrospect, he realized that the only way for the school to break free from this vicious cycle was by patient, regular and consistent conversations between members of the community, particularly between skilled adults and teenagers. There was no silver bullet. At that time, he felt, the school chaplain was, almost literally, a godsend. He was the trusted centrepoint: someone teenagers felt would listen to them, as they would listen to him.

Herb: What makes this issue so complex is that studies make it clear genuine suicidal intent is very difficult to assess.

Tony: So how can parents and teachers be ahead of the curve, rather than reacting helplessly?

Herb: Adults need to be sensitive to any signs of early mental disturbance: changes in personality, failure at school, hypochondriasis, social withdrawal and family problems. All these are important. So, too, are references to death and disaster, demonstrating a gloom-and-doom view of the world and a nihilistic approach to everything around them. Should there be a suicide attempt, the presence of a suicide note, whether anyone else was told about it, what precautions were taken to avoid discovery and the timing:

all need to be considered in order to identify motivation, knowledge of which can help professionals deal with the situation.

Tony: The key seems to be reacting early enough. There are good treatments available for anger management and drug and alcohol withdrawal, for example, and, as you have indicated, medication can work well. Often the most significant problem, however, is persuading over-16s (who have the legal right to determine their own actions) and their parents to engage.

Herb: If other routes are exhausted, in-patient treatment is essential. There is a great deal of evidence to support the success of this in preventing almost all ultimate suicidal actions.

Tony: It's worth noting that sometimes the suicide attempt in itself may have solved the problems, as a consequence of the attention the teenager receives. Because the situation is so serious, pretty much all school and personal conflicts are able to be discussed and, as such, resolved. I came across this when a group of four 16-year-olds took overdoses: one was serious about it; the other three were dabbling – two were seriously ill, but all survived. Subsequent conversation revealed that the motivation behind the serious attempt was, to an adult eye, relatively insignificant. All four were able to move on, but it was a terrible wake-up call to the adults involved. Even in retrospect, the school was hard pressed to identify warning signs. After the initial relief, it was a deeply unnerving experience for teachers and parents. There are no gilt-edged answers to issues involving depression and suicide.

Herb: No, but in most cases there's much that can be done. Where open communication between teenagers and adults is well established, it's highly likely that effective and timely help can be offered. That said, suicides have occurred despite all the efforts we've described. In such cases, family and friends will need support and understanding to help them avoid the likelihood of morbid grief reactions in picking up the pieces after such a seismic event. Life isn't easy.

SOME OTHER CONDITIONS

ME (myalgic encephalomyelitis), or CFS (chronic fatigue syndrome)

This occurs when the sufferer feels extreme tiredness and an inability to undertake ordinary daily activities, however mundane these might be. It can affect anyone, including young children, but the commonest age group is women aged 20 to 40. There is considerable debate within the medical community about the nature of the condition and its causes (and, indeed, its name, so it is now referred to as CFS/ME as a kind of compromise).

Triggers seem to include glandular fever or other viral illnesses, hormone imbalance, immunity problems and even genetics, as some families can have several members with the same symptomatology. There are also mental health issues including extreme stress and depression, but nothing particularly diagnostic. There is no specific test for the disorder, and the symptoms are similar to many common illnesses. These include joint and muscle pain, sleeping difficulties, sore throat without evidence of gland swelling, dizziness and vomiting, palpitations, headaches, nausea and so on. There is therefore no clear way, apart from observation and elimination of other possible disorders, to diagnose the condition.

With a singular lack of clarity about it, sufferers often have to deal not only with the symptoms, but also with the scepticism of those around them. Both family and school can prove unsympathetic. It can be hard not to express frustration, but for the sufferer and family the situation is real enough. The NHS website offers a CFS/ME helpline, as does the Royal College of Psychiatrists, meassociation.org.uk and others. The most recent study suggests the possibility of an over-active immune system.

ADHD, ASD and ADD

Tony: There are two areas of child and teenage behaviour that exercise parents mightily. They relate to the individual's ability to connect and respond to people around them appropriately. These days they both have names and acronyms: ADHD and ASD. Being able to give a medical label to behaviour other people might see as odd or even offensive has proved very helpful to many young people, because it helps them make sense of what they are experiencing. I sometimes think there is a tendency to play up to the label, or simply justify unacceptable activity. We need facts.

Herb: *Attention Deficit Hyperactivity Disorder* is said to be the commonest behavioural disorder in the United Kingdom and the United States, with up to about 5 per cent of schoolchildren being affected. Its symptoms are hyperactivity, impulsiveness and inattention. Most are diagnosed early and improve with age. The less common ADD (Attention Deficit Disorder) variant is less active and troublesome.

The condition is more common in children of low birth weight; who were born prematurely; where there are some genetic factors (for example, 75 per cent of identical twins will share the condition); and when the mother has been drinking, smoking or taking drugs during pregnancy. In other words, genetics, environment and social surroundings all play a role.

Boys outnumber girls by approximately three to one, and in as many as a third of cases the condition can extend into adulthood. Girls with ADHD are frequently seen as bubbly, friendly, talkative, helpful but scatty: likeable, but perhaps with rather more in the way of mood swings than others. Boys are more hyperactive and fidgety, and therefore rather more irritating to some teachers. Dealing with a hyperactive child is a test of good teaching – for example, allowing a hyperactive boy to stand spinning in circles in a classroom because that's the way he is best able to think.

ADHD occurs in all races, social classes and levels of IQ. If undiagnosed, there is a greater propensity in later life to undertake risky behaviours in matters of sex, drugs, etc., with implications for work performance, self-esteem and depression. This is critical in middle to late adolescence if there has been little treatment and understanding. In any event, there is a tendency to be far more accident-prone than normal, because of a lack of concentration and self-protectiveness. Repeated attendance at A&E units can become tiresome for parents.

Tony: As many as 10 per cent of children have some or all of the symptoms of ADHD. From a school perspective, we notice they have difficulty developing good relationships with others; an inability to focus, which can be misinterpreted as being uncaring or unreliable or deliberately forgetful (the 'butterfly brain'); they constantly interrupt, are fidgety, emotional and quickly forget, and wonder why everyone else is upset. They have an inability to prioritize and lack inhibition.

Herb: Concerned parents should be referred to a special needs professional or GP. Treatments can include drugs, behavioural therapy and family therapy if deemed necessary and, on the whole, results tend to be positive. There are associations with autistic spectrum disorders, Tourette's syndrome, obsessive-compulsive disorders and general anxiety. If possible, diagnosis is best from the age of six months onwards. There's no suggestion that excessive watching of television, sugar intake or poor parenting per se are root causes. Great strides have been made recently to destigmatize this condition. It's nobody's fault, but help is available.

Tony: That's been the case in schools as well, though teachers respond in very different ways, and not always helpfully. The important thing is to regard it as just one aspect of the human condition. All children can benefit from learning how to deal effectively and tolerantly with someone in their class whose behaviour is different. Much the same could be said of children with Asperger's, though that can be a more difficult issue to deal with in schools.

Herb: Asperger syndrome is a specific part of an entire range of disorders known as *Autism Spectrum Disorder (ASD)*. In all, the primary problems revolve around unusual reactions to social situations, behaviours, poor communication skills and general interests. In the UK, one in ten children has some degree of spectrum disorder: it is far commoner in boys than in girls, and half have some learning difficulties.

Tony: It seems to be experienced in very different ways. I've seen individuals talented in specific and often obsessional ways who work reasonably well, while others might withdraw into an almost zombie-like state.

Herb: The root cause appears to be an absence of normal filtering mechanisms. This means that there is a bombardment of stimuli from all sides, with noise being especially troubling. Some people are visually handicapped so that this includes colours as well. As a result, self-isolation seems the only way in which extreme cases can cope, which leads to enormous problems for the three-quarters of a million or so UK sufferers. Isolation extends to embarrassed carers, and it's especially exaggerated if a parent is also on the spectrum but has been able to develop coping strategies. Early diagnosis is really very important, possibly using DNA. Appropriate support can be structured, using treatments such as family work and group therapy. Registering a child as disabled can be useful, as it opens the door to a variety of allowances and information for parents and carers. There are also support groups for the family and for the individuals themselves.

Tony: By definition we are taking about a spectrum. What links are there to mental health issues and other disabilities?

Herb: Mental health issues are not necessarily part of the diagnosis, but learning disabilities might be. It is quite easy to be misdiagnosed because of the commonality with other disabilities such as dyspraxia (clumsiness), dyslexia (an inability to read and identify letters and figures) and ADHD. The primary problems are social interaction and communication. From an early age there is a lack of interest in others, delayed language development and unusual play activities which may be repetitive. Obsessive features are prominent and can be irritating. It's probably worth noting that the latest evidence indicates very young children watching television to excess have a much higher incidence of ADHD than would otherwise be expected.

Tony: In school, we notice that teenagers with ASD tend to avoid eye contact and seem to register few emotive facial expressions. More strikingly, they can't understand or read the expressions of other people, and they ignore non-verbal cues. This translates as indifference and rudeness, which makes it very hard for the individual to be accepted.

Herb: We shouldn't forget that high-functioning autism has been part of the genius of some amazing people, like Archimedes, Einstein and even George Washington. It's sometimes called the 'genius gene'.

Tony: That's true, but it doesn't detract from the difficulties they can experience dealing with the people around them. Routines are essential for them, and when their observation is thwarted it can cause considerable distress. This, in turn, can lead to frustration in school. Small wonder that ASD teenagers can be isolated and depressed as a consequence. School can be an over-whelming and confusing place, and it's not hard to see why an ASD teenager might lash out. As so often, training school staff effectively is the key.

Herb: When it comes to seeking advice, parents would be well advised to contact MENCAP, a remarkable and effective charity.

Serious psychiatric conditions such as schizophrenia, bipolar or manic-depressive disorder and brain damage are not really subjects for discussion in this book. They all require medical interventions and constant oversight.

8

Addictions

Herb: Personally, I regard addiction of any kind as ultimately misery cloaked and disguised as pleasure, however fleeting and transient it might be, with the potential need to return again and again to an activity which is potentially dangerous.

Tony: That's a pretty good definition, but perhaps at the outset we should distinguish between addiction and habit, which are often confused or used as synonyms.

Habits, in the main, are rather benign. We should encourage our children to develop good habits: harnessing the efficiency and comfort of routines, being in the habit of taking exercise at certain times, having regular mealtimes and so on. Sometimes habits can become deeply engrained and even damaging, and may prove difficult to break, but it is possible to interrupt them without too much emotional distress.

Herb: Addictions are a very different breed. They have been described as behaviours which reverse overwhelming feelings of helplessness and arise from related actions which become virtually impossible to avoid or control. There is a view that 'Sniff, snort, swallow and all will be well.' This gives a temporary relief from whatever troubles are being experienced. Inevitably, the first steps towards relieving emotional pain end up creating it. We readily associate addiction with drugs and alcohol, but it can apply just as much with a whole range of things, like excessive dieting, exercising and even eating.

WHAT TO LOOK OUT FOR: THE COMMON, ESSENTIAL FEATURES OF ADDICTIONS

1 Thinking about an activity all the time, such as smartphone usage.
2 Ever-increasing engagement in the activity in order to feel satisfied.
3 Actions becoming beyond the ability of the individual to control.
4 Becoming restless, irritable and extremely anxious whenever attempting to stop the activity.
5 Escaping from reality.
6 Constantly lying in order to conceal the extent of usage.
7 Jeopardizing relationships and jobs or studies.
8 Showing increasingly marked withdrawal symptoms.
9 Extending beyond the original intention – e.g. spending much more time or having a greater dosage than anticipated.
10 Being in denial and repeatedly seeking self-assurance ('I can stop at any time').

Tony: This checklist is useful at home and school. To put things in perspective, many teenagers will experiment, few will become addicted users; but one can lead to the other with surprising ease. There's a wide range of addictive substances, from caffeine, tobacco and alcohol to cannabis and hard drugs. There's also a range of addictive patterns of behaviour, from obsessive exercising to gaming and gambling. With so many dangers out there, what is it that's so attractive about these activities? It seems that the pull of the pack and the need to belong are central.

Herb: That's certainly part of it, but it's also about feeling good, increasing performance and, particularly for teenagers, cocking a snook at authority – all part of adolescent risk-taking. Addiction occurs when there are changes in the brain. This might be due to a wide variety of influences, which could include abuse or trauma of any kind, genetics, lack of supervision, as well as the powerful influence of friends, both real and virtual.

Tony: In the teenage years there can be a pleasure in secretiveness and romance about behaviour that leads to addiction. The covert mystery of the drugs world, for example. That's why it's good for teenagers to have information, not least about the drugs business, which in some ways is a business like any other, with producers, suppliers and consumers. People are in it to make money: there is no hint of the romance which some teenagers feel.

One of the frightening aspects of the drugs market is the lack of quality control. Most talks to teenagers about drugs have little impact: they hear what they want to hear. One that hit home was the reformed drug addict who gave a teenager a small bag of cannabis and asked him to pass it down the row. It went through ten pairs of hands. He asked the tenth whether she would now use it. A drug user has no idea how many hands have interfered with the substance, how many times it has been adulterated with something like brick dust – just how unreliably dangerous it could be. In short, a typical teenage drugs consumer has no idea what it is he or she is buying and using.

Herb: It is interesting, though, that there seems to be a shift in attitude. A recent survey of 1,000 university students has revealed that nearly three-quarters of them have not taken illegal drugs during the time of their studies. Most believe that drug-taking affects mental health and contributes to criminality.

Tony: That may be true of universities, but there are many communities where drug-taking is part and parcel of normal life and linked, for example, with teenage knife crime in areas of London.

Herb: Yet we shouldn't lose sight of the progress that is being made. With alcohol use, for example: 50 per cent of 16-year-old males drank weekly in 2002; that figure was down to 10 per cent in 2014. It has also declined in the 18–24 age group. In fact, according to the WHO, teenage drinking has declined in England more than in any other EU country. In a recent Eventbrite study, only 10 per cent of teenagers rate getting drunk as 'cool': 40 per cent now think it is embarrassing. The old distinction that in Britain people laugh with you when you are drunk, but at you on the continent, no longer applies.

Tony: You're right to highlight the positive, but humans have a propensity to addiction. The Global Commission on Drug Policy states that 'taking substances to alter one's mind seems to be a universal impulse, seen in almost all countries around the world and across history.' It has always seemed to me counterproductive to make a moral issue out of drug use, which is how schools certainly used to react.

The heroic no-tolerance approach only served to make the subject taboo and even more attractive to teenagers.

Herb: Stigmatization and labelling are still commonplace: junkies are subhuman; crack addicts are scum. This simply makes matters worse because they are then less likely to seek help. However tough it can be, it's almost always possible to turn a drug addiction around and create a new and positive set of habits.

Tony: We should always take the long view and do what is best for the person concerned, but part of that approach is having very clear lines with teenagers and sticking to them. If nature abhors a vacuum, then teenagers flounder in uncertainly. We have already talked about the tendency towards black-and-white thinking in the developing adolescent brain. The approach I would take is this:

1 If a pupil is found in school using, possessing or selling illegal drugs, they must go: they have forfeited their place in the school and there should be no exceptions. That clarity is essential. Expulsion is not the end of the world.

   Teenagers can have a fresh start, face up to their situation and end up doing very well. It won't work every time, but there are plenty of examples where it has. Parents need to have equally clear lines about family expectations with a sanction: something serious and followed through.

2 Just as important, however, is teenagers' knowledge that there is openness and support from school and parents. This means giving good factual information, discussing the challenges and pitfalls of the social scene, responding sympathetically to their concerns

about their friends and themselves without making judgments, but pointing out the dangers.

There is a misguided small minority of parents who actually encourage their children in drug abuse, sometimes with hard drugs. It beggars belief, but it happens at all levels of society. The vast majority, however, want a healthy life for their children. They are, rightly, confident about their child's future, even if it's a confidence laced with fear. The antidote to fear in this situation is knowledge.

TOBACCO

The dangers of smoking are very well known and proven around the world, and especially in the English-speaking part. Yet tobacco remains the leading cause of death worldwide, with over seven million people dying annually because of it. The good news in the UK is the dramatic fall in tobacco use among teenagers: it has ceased to be seen as attractive. Using e-cigarettes is seen by some teenagers as a safe alternative but, while vaping is useful in reducing smoking-related illnesses, it is not yet proven to be safe, as many think. As well as nicotine, several other toxic substances are emitted which have yet to be fully evaluated. Ironically, starting with vaping can lead to smoking in earnest. As far as the safety of these substances is concerned, the jury is still out. There is an additional, related issue: as rates of smoking have dropped, so rates of obesity in teenagers have risen sharply. Tobacco suppresses appetite.

POPPERS (LIQUID GOLD, AMYL OR BUTYL NITRATE)

These are not illegal to possess or buy. They're often sold in joke or sex shops, but also in pubs, clubs and sometimes the music or clothes shops young people frequent. Usually made from amyl nitrate, and once used in breakable capsules for heart disease, these are seen as inexpensive and safe party-mood drugs, especially among the young. Poppers can be a routine part of teenage weekend conversation. There are, however, the inevitable side effects: in this case, allergic skin problems, breathing difficulties and glaucoma, potentially leading to blindness. As a muscle relaxant, poppers are thought to intensify sexual experience.

SOLVENTS (AEROSOLS, GASES, GLUES ETC.)

Similarly, it's not illegal to possess, use or buy solvents at any age, although it is an offence for a shopkeeper to sell them to an under-18-year-old if they know they are to be used for intoxication. VSA (Volatile Substance Abuse) describes the misuse of common substances like glue, gases and aerosols. Instant suffocation and death are not uncommon, whether as a consequence of a direct chemical effect or from vomiting and choking, but the long-term damage is to other organs, including the brain. As with much secretive use of drugs, VSA developed its own language – 'huffing', 'sniffing' and 'dusting' being part of the lexicon. VSA tends to be home-based, often using butane gas, and is less marked as a major issue in and around schools. Drugwise is a valuable helpsite.

NITROUS OXIDE (ALSO KNOWN AS NITROUS)

This is widely used as a simple anaesthetic, commonly by dentists providing pain and anxiety relief. It was labelled laughing gas by Humphrey Davy because of the euphoria it produces. This antique treatment (it has been around for about 300 years) is still widely used in clubs and at parties because it is easy to purchase, though it's illegal for anything other than professional use. The UK is the highest user, according to one survey: evidence can frequently be seen on pavements and in school corridors in the form of little silver canisters. It is a friendly-seeming gas that is used in balloons and, as it's not a psychoactive substance, is not as toxic as others, but side-effects include confusion, hallucinations, facial numbness and vitamin B12 depletion!

ALCOHOL

Still the most socially acceptable drug. There is a prevalent view that children can learn to drink responsibly by being allowed to have diluted alcohol at a young age. This is often advocated while casting an eye across to our neighbours in France. Yet a recent *Lancet* article, involving a study of 2000 12- to 18-year-olds tracked for 6 years, notes that there were no benefits to introducing alcohol at home: it only seems to encourage them to drink elsewhere. Alcohol-related harm is much higher in children who have been given alcohol by their parents. AUD (Alcohol Use Disorder) is well described in the DSM–5. A London study has revealed that half of British teenagers start drinking by the age of 14, and 10 per cent of the 11,000 surveyed have at least 5 alcoholic drinks in one sitting.

It is the addiction to binge drinking that is the most worrying feature, particularly with girls. The WHO notes that teenage girls in England, Scotland and Wales occupy 3 of the top 6 slots in the 36-nation European League. British girls actually drink less than previous generations, but binge more. Girls themselves attribute this to the increasing stress of life and to the promotion of sweeter, fizzier drinks.

While it is perhaps comforting to see drinking as just part of the process of adolescent push-back – and that is certainly part of the motivation – alcohol has been shown to lead to experimentation with other drugs, as well as anti-social behaviour, vandalism and theft. Given that the Millennium Cohort Study notes that substance abuse increases sharply between the ages of 11 and 14, schools and parents need to be alert to what is going on. Advice about prevention has tended to be school-focused. There is a good case for schools spending more time helping parents understand the situation, not least by drawing to their attention the prevalence of apps that encourage binge drinking. In return, schools need to be robust with the small number of parents who seek to curry favour by encouraging their children and their friends to drink. This is a dereliction of parenting and has led to some disastrous consequences.

At university level, Alcoholics Anonymous report an increase in the number of university-age problem drinkers attending meetings. Some universities, like Cardiff, offer therapeutic sessions for self-referring students who are concerned about themselves. We are at the stage where there is a dawning acceptance of the need for attention to mental health, both from the individual and public bodies. There is still a long way to go.

THE MISUSE OF DRUGS ACT

It's worth being reminded about the legal framework for drugs in the UK. In essence, there are three classes of drug covered by the act. Possession, supply and use of premises are offences.

Group A, deemed the most harmful, contains cocaine, ecstasy, crystal meth, opioids such as heroin etc.

Group B includes barbiturates, cannabis, ketamine, amphetamines.

Group C includes steroids, benzodiazepines etc.

CANNABIS

In all its forms, with many different names and new synthetic derivatives, marijuana is smoked by at least a quarter of those aged under 40 in the US and in all probability in the UK as well. These drugs interfere with the natural pleasure-and-reward system of the brain, hence leading to dependence. All forms of cannabis impact to a greater or lesser degree on the developing brain, particularly attention, learning and memory. But perhaps the most important fact for parents to take on board is that the cannabis sold today is a very great deal stronger than in previous generations: up to *40 times stronger* than in the Summer of Love in the 60s.

The most potent variants are extremely dangerous. Skunk, four times stronger than the basic variety, is sinister: long-term use is strongly associated with brain damage and severe psychosis and paranoia. It appears to be the most widely sold drug on our streets. Active compounds which are so addictive include tetrahydrocannabinol (THC), cannabinol and cannabidiol which regulate mood, appetite, memory and the way pain is interpreted. Unlike tobacco, which is destructive in bodily terms, these compounds hammer the brain, but the dangers are nowhere near as widely disseminated as for tobacco. Horror stories appear in the press from time to time and are then forgotten. Cannabis almost certainly has many compounds that could prove useful medically. It is being researched in labs worldwide for its potential use in the treatment of epilepsy, cancer and other diseases, and also as an anxiolytic (reducing anxiety), but there is not yet conclusive evidence. At present the adverse effects of cannabis outweigh the positive.

Nonetheless, 29 states in the US and a growing number of countries, mainly in Europe, permit medical and recreational use. Yet there are two important issues to consider. First, 'gateway drugs' is the term used to describe the way commonly used drugs can lead to dependence on more serious ones. Cannabis confections are widely available, such as cakes and sweets, and seem safe, but it has been proved that they can be the precursor to a more dangerous cannabis habit, which can in turn lead to another level of drug use. Second, younger teenagers are at particular risk. Recent Canadian studies show that those using cannabis under the age of 15 are 66 per cent more likely to become addicts. This compares with 44 per cent who start at age 17. At the very least, we should recognize that cannabis is not without significant risk.

At the most dangerous end of the cannabis scale are cannabinoids (synthetic alternatives to cannabis like spice that have been manufactured in a laboratory), known as the 'zombie' drugs. These are really sinister, and the effect on those who take them is often very unpredictable behaviour, with a range of toxic symptoms and potentially devastating effects on the nervous and cardiovascular systems. These so-called 'legal highs' are seen by some to be harmless. They are not. As a smokeable mixture of herbs and synthetic psychoactive drugs, Spice can be classified as aromatherapy, but it is frequently used in a very different way. Benzo, Summer Haze, K2, Fury and a host of others involve so much mixing that overdoses are becoming harder to deal with: not knowing what they have actually used reduces the accuracy of specific treatments.

There are ways back. It's comforting for parents, and the user, to know that even 72 hours of abstinence can lead to some cognitive recovery.

OPIOIDS

The commonest is codeine, easily obtained over the counter in painkillers, hence widely abused.

Opium and morphine are in the same family. Overdosing leads to confusion, drowsiness and slow breathing, which is very dangerous. It is among the most used drugs in suicide attempts, but medications to reverse the effects are available and effective if used early enough.

Heroin (diamorphine) produces even more intense effects. Usage is signalled by obvious injection marks. Cravings are so powerful, and withdrawal symptoms so appalling, that users will take extreme measures to obtain their fix. Very different from the effect of normally produced endorphins.

COCAINE AND OTHER STIMULANTS

These include the amphetamines, one of which is MDMA (Ecstasy), bought as powder or tablets or liquid. These drugs are valuable in treating ADHD (Attention Deficit Hyperactivity Disorder), but are also misused as a recreational drug or to keep awake for whatever reason. Cocaine is used as a local anaesthetic, but this is quite rare. As a street drug it is a white powder (crack, blow, snow, coke etc), rarely sold in pure form but mixed with a variety of interesting substances, some of which are toxic. Dosage can therefore be anything at all, from exceptionally strong to almost nothing at all. It is hard, if not impossible, to know exactly what it is you are taking. It is smoked, inhaled, rubbed on gums or injected. It produces dopamine and is therefore very pleasurable. As with all other drugs of addiction, withdrawal can be dangerous and very distressing.

According to the Home Office, usage among the wealthiest sectors is at a 10-year high in England and Wales. Too many people believe that cocaine is harmless. It isn't. Indeed, despite cocaine's common usage, and its being therefore deemed harmless by some, there is no doubt that it warrants being placed in the Class A drug grouping.

ANABOLIC STEROIDS

These are easily bought on the internet or even illegally in gyms. They are attractive mostly to boys and young men as they increase desirable body bulk, but are very addictive and potentially deadly. For adolescent boys using them to bulk up is also a way of improving their self-perception. As performance-enhancing drugs they are therefore tested for in competition to eliminate unfair advantage. They are available as tablets, creams and injections.

This is a new drug challenge for schools. Almost by definition, using anabolic steroids is not seen by teenagers as adolescent rebellion or, indeed, as taking a drug at all. But side effects include acne, baldness, strokes, heart attacks and serious psychological effects such as paranoia, delusions, hypomania and severe aggression. If used before puberty, physical growth is inhibited.

ENERGY DRINKS

These are all caffeine-based, but with far higher doses than you would find in coffee, tea or chocolate. Almost all contain large quantities of sugar – up to 20 teaspoons per bottle. Tooth decay, Type 2 diabetes and obesity might be the end result. All are used as stimulants and pick-me-ups by people who want to stay awake or alert – for gaming, study, sporting activity and so on. It is believed about two-thirds of older teenagers regularly consume them.

'HAPPY HORMONES'

These are not manufactured drugs taken by adolescents to try and deliberately alter their mood. They are naturally occurring compounds in our brains that are mood-altering in various ways whether we like it or not. It is desirable to be aware of their potential effects, and when they are likely to be triggered.

Dopamine drives us to achieve goals and experience the pleasure that follows. Low levels can lead to dissatisfaction, lack of enthusiasm and even desperation. A dopamine high can sometimes tip over into a hangover-like low mood.

Oxytocin has been referred to as the 'cuddle hormone', because of the positive effect it has on relationships. It is released in sexual activity, physical intimacy such as hugging and kissing, even shaking hands warmly; and through exhibiting friendship. Intimacy, trust and fidelity can be seen to flow from hormone release. Incidentally, it is also said to strengthen the immune system and improve cardiovascular function.

Serotonin makes people feel good about themselves and the world at large. Vitamin D production, mainly from the sun and a healthy diet, increases output, as do good social experiences and a feeling of belonging. It follows that social isolation and a feeling of abandonment lead to a reduction in serotonin production. Our brains can produce serotonin in response to positive memories, whether real or imagined, and quiet reflection can lead to an increase in the hormone.

Endorphins is the shortened name of the internally produced morphine-like substances referred to as endomorphines. These hormones are stress-reducing and lead to a much desired high. They reduce anxiety, are pain-relieving and, in high doses, provide powerful sedatives. Having fun and laughing, or taking enjoyable exercise, are ways to increase endorphin output. So do special smells, familiar foods, such as coffee and chocolate, and aromatherapy. Sniffing lavender as an oil or an ointment is a well-known relaxant.

OTHERS

Experience shows that few users are purists. Anything deemed to have a pleasurable effect, whether physical or psychological, goes into the mix. There are a great many other substances of abuse, too many to mention, but here are two of particular note.

Xanax (alprazolam) is one of the benzodiazepine group, and is prescribed for anxiety. It is being increasingly used by teenagers, and more so by university students, who can buy from anonymized websites. Benzodiazepines act very quickly, and can therefore be effective with panic attacks and phobias. Where treatment is not readily available, as is still too often the case at university, self-medicated usage soars. This drug is valuable, but toxic.

Gamma-hydroxybutyrate (GHB), often known as G, is popular with clubbers, especially women, and with the LGBT community as a 'chem-sex' drug, functioning as a powerful disinhibitor, It rapidly leads to euphoria and seems not to have side-effects. But if mixed with alcohol It can lead to coma within minutes, and was the original rape drug, being tasteless and odourless and easily slipped into a drink.

GHB was developed 60 years ago as an anaesthetic and a treatment for narcolepsy, and thus has the apparent imprimatur of being a medical and 'pure' drug. Yet it is one of the most dangerous drugs a young person could possibly use. It's now referred to as 'liquid Ecstasy', and kills people – indeed, it seems to have replaced Ecstasy tablets as the most widely used drug, particularly in clubbing culture.

COUNTY LINES

A worrying development has been the way drug gangs are exploiting young people, using children as young as 12 to move drugs and money for them around the country, usually by train or coach. Initial contact is often made through a form of grooming on social media, backed up by the threat of violence: firearms, knives and acid have been used as enforcers. The most common drugs involved are heroin, cocaine, ecstasy, cannabis, amphetamines and spice. As with much of the drugs world, it has created its own language. 'Going county' is the most popular term for the whole activity. 'Trapping', 'trap house', 'trap line' and 'cuckooing' are words that should trigger alarm. Using children as carriers ('muling') is a modern form of enslavement. The website fearless.org covers this ground.

GAMING

Tony: Who would have thought that simple black-and-white ping-pong game of old, which is my memory of the very first computer game, would have developed into such a billion-dollar industry affecting virtually all societies and most age groups throughout the world?

Herb: It has become so pervasive and threatening to some that the WHO has felt it necessary to classify Gaming Disorder as a disease, ICD-11. By creating a cycle of reward phenomena that can interfere with all aspects of personality development, gaming can become an addiction spreading into the lives of all members of the family, through computer games at home and on the internet.

Tony: But, as with many things, in the right 'dose' at the right time and in the right place, gaming is a pleasurable pastime and can be put to good use. Indeed, I've seen how gaming can divert self-centred negative thinking towards something relatively healthy, and how it be a positive experience to the socially isolated. Huddersfield University are trailing a pro-social game to be used in schools, aimed at 14- to 18-year-olds, that rewards conscientious behaviour and sets an alarm for the coercive and violent aspects of social media, including grooming. Their research has revealed that aggressive games can lead to violent behaviour and 'socially conscientious' games can actually improve patterns of behaviour.

Herb: There's a lot that can go wrong, though. The commercial market seems to be a free-for-all. The Chinese, the world's biggest nation of gamers with some 500 million users, producing £300 billion in profits, have recently set up censorship committees and found ethics violations in all 20 of the first set of games they reviewed.

Tony: I don't doubt that. Yet there are positive advantages. The improvement that can be made in hand-eye co-ordination and brain connect, for example, is now influencing the way the military conduct their recruitment. There's also the sharpening of split-second decision-making, a skill that can be rapidly and effective taught. You can actually see young people improving their problem-solving ability through gaming, and it can benefit cognitive functioning overall: memory, attention, reasoning, processing information and so on. It's only relatively recently that schools have begun to see the potential in gaming. We are potentially on the cusp of a real boost to the business of learning.

Herb: It works because most games give emotional satisfaction, with the reward centres of the brain being activated, leading to increased perseverance, and this, of course, is also part of the problem. Sexual and violent themes catch the gamer on the reward/perseverance hook as well.

It's not that sex and violence in games necessarily lead to moral confusion and decline. Indeed, some studies have shown that watching violent films or games has the opposite effect to what might be expected: assault levels actually fall. The craze for Fortnite, a game where the aim is to be the last man standing, having wiped out everyone else, is not so different to a Tom and Jerry cartoon. The issue is the hook of addiction – and the fact that sexual and violent themes don't develop cognitive skills in anything like the same way as some other games. The hook has become a significant issue. One London NHS Trust is now pioneering an internet addiction centre along the lines of those in the Far East and America.

Tony: In any event, games are here to stay, and have many benefits. What is required both at school and in the family is control and selectivity. This is not at all easy to achieve. So . . .

SOME TIPS:

- Attempt to know what is being viewed on television, internet or gaming. It never fails to amaze both of us that there are parents who don't even make the effort to find out
- Try to enforce time limits
- Don't allow devices in the bedroom
- Check surreptitiously to be sure
- Attempt a discussion about the game ('What is so good about it?') and the feelings it engenders ('Does it make you feel better, depressed, angry, happy, relaxed?')
- Try to obtain information from friends, school or other parents (and the web itself) about the desirability or otherwise of any particular game

And don't forget the Hypocrite Rule. Parents are role models, like it or not: adults over-using screens are hardly setting a good example.

Useful websites for parents: UKAT (UK); Netease (China)

GAMBLING

Tony: Gambling is another very lucrative business and well-established in our culture – the flutter on the horses or a punt at the football. For many years gambling has been seen as harmless enough with just a few outliers: poor souls who have got themselves into difficulty. What has changed, and made the potential for major problems much greater, has been the speed of personal contact through the smartphone. There is a worryingly large number of gambling websites that don't require proof of age.

Herb: One piece of research suggests that about half of 16-year-olds use their betting apps surreptitiously. This can lead to them slipping into a quagmire of theft from home, which can then then be exploited. Boys seem to gamble twice as much as girls. The dopamine release system affords enormous pleasure for even the smallest win, something well known to lottery card companies.

Tony: It's a growing international problem. China has established hundreds of internet addiction therapy centres with a rather cold-turkey approach, sufficient to make readmission an unattractive prospect. The Chinese authorities are well aware what they are facing.

Herb: The Chinese approach is not the only way forward. Support groups, therapy and online advice can all help. Gambling Anonymous is like its Alcoholic counterpart, offering support both for the parent and the young people themselves. Changing to a traditional call-and-receive phone, whatever the opposition, can be useful – and probably cheaper!

WHAT PARENTS CAN DO

With any child at any time, it's a very good thing to create a climate in which issues of addiction are discussed. Tackle the scene well before there's even a hint that there's a problem. For example, 'I've been reading about . . .' can be a prompt for a general discussion. Children need to know their parents are reasonably clued up about the things going on in their lives. And try to be open, too: 'I'm always willing to talk about . . .' Don't necessarily expect a positive, or indeed any, response to begin with.

Teenagers can feel irked or embarrassed that their parents are on their territory, but gentle persistence often pays dividends. Don't give up! If you do have concerns about your child's behaviour, then:

1 Identify the problem. Be certain of your facts.
2 Challenge your child. Expect to be deceived, at least initially. Expect outrage. You can talk about warning signals – 'We're not stupid.'
3 This is a very stressful situation for most parents, so be calm and take stock. Try to arrive at a shared plan of action before a third party is involved.
4 That third party may well be a confidential counsellor or, indeed, the school. Many parents will feel wary about this, but a good school will be open-minded and helpful. In any event, make sure the ten points under 'What to look out for' are discussed in detail.
5 What you are aiming for is not a quick-fix solution, but a plan with a positive sense of direction. The whole family will need to be considered and involved, as appropriate.
6 If there really is no sense of a plan at all, you face tough decisions, which may even include asking a child to leave home, perhaps to live with a relative, especially if there are other children to consider.

The NHS and Partnership for Drug-Free Kids websites offer good advice to parents about dealing with a suspicion or evidence of children's drug use. Much of this advice is applicable to other addictions. Other useful websites are provided by the Royal College of Psychiatrists and Young Minds.

When young people are worried about parental substance abuse, narconon.org/drug addiction can be valuable.

9

Screenagers

Herb: Can you remember a time when everyone actually made eye contact, with a smile, fully aware of their environment? All gone, pretty much. Screens are everywhere. They seem to be permanently with us: in our living rooms, our bedrooms, on public transport – almost anywhere one cares to look. Televisions, computers, tablets, smartphones, wristwatches are omnipresent, covering virtually all spheres of human activity. TVs have largely been displaced by smaller, portable electronic devices which are always to hand. A combination of accessibility and sheer power has transformed the way we communicate and access information.

Tony: It's certainly a radically different view of the world, and really we are only glimpsing its ramifications. As far as young people are concerned, the primary use appears to be for their social connections. The technology is also used for information and academic purposes, but these are not nearly as attractive as gaming or Instagram. Schools are quite some way behind. There are schools that expect their pupils to bring in tablets or smartphones for academic use but then barely use them, which leaves many parents feeling their children are being made vulnerable to a potential new distraction for little discernible benefit. On the other hand, when schools give parents specific advice about the smartphones and tablets that are appropriate for their children, parents will often still buy the unnecessarily powerful, fashionable version. You have a sense that technology is directing the way we live, rather than being used as just a useful tool.

Herb: We've known for some while that, on the whole, when it comes to the cyber world young people are far in advance of most adults. I've read that care homes are being asked to provide free wi-fi so grandchildren will visit! Note the power of the surrogate-parent-in-the-pocket! Young people are trailblazers in a way, intuitively searching for new methods, new thought processes, new words. You're a schoolmaster: you must know what these mean: 'butters', 'on point', 'curve', 'stand', 'fleeck', 'sheg' . . .?

Tony: No, I don't and even if I did, that knowledge would be redundant by next week!

Herb: Me neither. I think they mean something on the lines of: 'attractive', 'perfection', 'rejecting advances', 'being a fan', 'cool and good', 'embarrassed' . . . but I take your point.

Tony: It's as though a whole dimension of the adult world has been sidelined and forgotten, and is being reinvented according to new rules, however fleeting and evanescent these might be. Young people are presented with a world of extraordinary opportunity and excitement. Smartphones can be a social crutch, too, compensating for awkwardness – just reach for the magic lifeline and play with it.

Herb: Ultimately, like everything else, the impact of the screen depends on the dose. The four-letter word in this instance is TIME! A smartphone can turn from being a good thing to a bad thing to a very bad thing.

Tony: But it does offer many good things: literally a lifesaver in emergencies, great for contacting people easily all around the world and for dealing with the routines of everyday life, from banking to watching video material to booking holidays, navigating journeys and accessing news. It's also a phenomenal resource for information: a colleague of mine once described it as being 'the library of Alexandria in your pocket'. It's also a truly remarkable resource for self-directed learning. The list goes on and on. Perhaps we are already recognizing that this information revolution is marking a step-change in the development of humankind.

Herb: The inevitable question that arises relates to balance. Do the positive elements outweigh the negative, given that so much is changing so rapidly that it is almost impossible to envisage what the future holds? One of the major difficulties young people experience is the way the Internet seems to provide a pathway towards a perfect existence. It therefore follows that they might readily believe that if they do not keep a constant eye on what the mobile phone is transmitting to their brains, everything in their lives will go wrong – they will be left out, experiences will be negative and almost everything that seems to be worthwhile will come adrift.

Tony: What strikes me is not so much the pursuit of perfection as the sheer pervasiveness of the internet. There is a new term that describes the way many individuals feel lost and abandoned when the phone is not immediately to hand. *Nomophobia*, fear of no mobile, is seen to affect all ages in the same way. There is now even an online way of checking whether you have it!

Herb: Yes, it would be amusing were it not for the fact that there is now distinct evidence it's addictive and leads to mental and physical disturbances, such as separation anxiety and panic attacks, with high blood pressure and increased heart rate. Ofcom data for August 2018 reveals that almost 20 per cent of 16- to 24-year-olds spend 7 hours each day online. As one might expect, there's a significant generational divide: whereas 1 per cent of over-65s spend 50 hours a week online, that number rises to 18 per cent for 16- to 24-year-olds. It seems as if it's impossible to combat this tidal wave, but there are ways. Ofcom also states that Brits check their mobile phones every 12 minutes and are on-line for 24 hours per week on average. Girls use social media more than boys. Perhaps surprisingly, fewer than 15 per cent of adults never use the internet.

Tony: Sometimes the best way to deal with things is the simplest way. While it seems to me an axiom of good education that young people should learn and discover for themselves, and while many of them will indeed sort out the most beneficial use of the internet and social media, all teenagers and younger children can be relieved when pressure is removed from them for a time. Having a ban on phones at certain periods of the day, for example, can take steam out of the pressure cooker. This applies as much at home as it does in school. One American head imposed a curfew, which was met with initial grumbling, then relief, as pupils chose to take responsibility for policing their iPhone-free world. He was privately delighted when in an absent moment he reached for his own mobile phone and his pupils demanded it be confiscated!

Herb: That's a good example of humanity triumphing over technology – intrusion in reverse!

Tony: There was an interesting footnote. The pupils at that school decided to create a Handshaking Club. The rule imposed was that when anybody in the school community met, they would share a handshake and eye contact: not a single tweet!

Herb: Another example of policing self-discipline is encouraging them to use a lockable, time-released pouch. It leads to periods when there is enforced respite from inevitable texting, checking Facebook, Snapchat and all the rest. This is an approach now being used in some schools, and by some parents, too.

Tony: But the underlying fact is that there has to be a willingness on the part of individuals to allow themselves to be nudged into self-discipline. There are ways round any system. In practice, I've found that many young people will understand the issues when explained clearly, and be prepared to moderate their use of smartphones. There will always be those who will find it hard or impossible or just don't want to listen. What we are talking about here is the essence of human communication.

Herb: Communication is the key word, but we know that teenagers spend less and less time in personal interactions and less time on hobbies and activities, too, unless they are accessed through the portal of their smartphones. What is notable, though, is that there has been a marked increase in loneliness over the past five years, as described in many studies of young people. This is linked to an upsurge in the incidence of depression, which seems to be increasing at an alarming rate. Because smartphone-as-a-way-of-life was not an experience for their parents, it's hard for them to understand that the vast majority of young people can't remember a time in their lives when there wasn't one available for instant use.

Tony: Emotional immaturity persists far longer than it used to. It's easy enough for parents and teachers to feel worried that children might be being exposed to bad things online, but Professor Jean Twenge exposes a different, but equally worrying phenomenon. Young people who live their lives through a smartphone inhabit a world protected from many broader realities. They become less independent and resilient. Algorithms point them in particular directions, generally reinforcing their limited worldview. They can become passionate about what they deem to be unfair and unequal, but can't or won't cope with alternative viewpoints. We see this in universities, with the spread of the practice of 'no-platforming' speakers held to be beyond the pale. I find this deeply worrying. It cuts to the quick of what education should be: well-informed, independent minds testing hypotheses and views through constructive debate and argument. It seems there may be a link between smartphone and snowflake cultures.

Herb: What I find worrying is the speed with which universities seem to be yielding too readily to suppression of free speech. There is evidence that the government is beginning to confront this. Lines need to be drawn and adhered to, with plenty of explanation about the reasons why.

Tony: You're describing good parenting!

Herb: You mention young people spending less time going out with friends and engaging in traditional activities, but there is another aspect to it. They are engaging less in direct sex. This may be in part due to internet porn. While there are examples of young people enacting a distorted view of sexual performance and relationships, there is also some evidence that seeing sex online is dealing with their normal urges. Certainly the birthrate among young people is at an all-time low, though this may be due to proper prophylaxis as well as the morning-after pill; we don't know at this stage. It's likely that unwanted loneliness and desired aloneness play a role here, too.

Tony: Another element is experience of adult work. There are far fewer jobs available for teenagers these days. Parents frequently complain that part-time or Saturday work is just not available any more. There may be a number of reasons for this, not least much tighter rules around safeguarding, but the net effect is reducing opportunities for young people to experience a different kind of social life, as well as learn something about accountability and responsibility. Earning even a pittance for work helps shape self-worth and value. Inevitably, we can't ignore the pull of the screen: gaming can be rather more fun than work.

Herb: We have touched on a number of issues, but what is clear is that levels of unhappiness are going up. This seems to correlate directly with screen usage. It's a one-way phenomenon: excessive use equals increased depression, but depression does not necessarily lead to excessive use of smartphones. There is also a strong link to the incidence of deliberate self-harm, which is very much on the increase. There are many studies that show the extent to which young people view their smartphone as an extension of their body. A large minority sleep with their phone under the pillow and check it frequently, sometimes as much as ten times a night, often with the excuse that it is their clock and alarm, and without it they cannot get up in time for school.

Tony: It's sometimes hard for families to know what they should be doing to tackle something that may very well be damaging the welfare of their children. Some adopt strict curfews for phone use, but many find it difficult. Some have tried banning phones in the bedroom, but allowing use of social media through a television. The trouble with what might appear punitive reactions is that they can stimulate desire even more. To me the best route is through broad-ranging discussion that is as open as possible, ranging from big-picture issues, like the dangers of international cyber-conflict, to the personal stuff, like social responsibility or some science around the damage caused by persistent blue light. Take some of the furtive mystery out of it.

Herb: The online world is glamorous: fame and fortune can be achieved overnight. Yet it's highly unlikely that most young people using the internet are more than dimly aware of the extent to which it is a money-making exercise for large corporations or even individual vloggers – young people with vast internet followings who use product placement for financial gain. Advertisements have leapt from the magazine to the screen and, as a result, have become constant and persistent, with ever-increasing pressure to buy expensive items or do things which in the ordinary course of events would have been deemed unacceptable not that long ago. Very few adults fully understand the extent to which the lives of a whole generation have been taken over by smartphones.

Tony: As in all aspects of parenting, adults need to be good role models. It's interesting how parents who are sensitive to the need to set a good example in most aspects of life unwittingly fall at the smartphone hurdle. Rather like the American headmaster, they can allow themselves to be absorbed in their own smartphones, sometimes to the exclusion of everything else – and children notice. You can see whole families in a restaurant, each member engrossed in their own phone. The curfew route will only really work if it applies to the whole family.

Herb: That's such an important point. The old adage 'Do as I say, not as I do' has to be looked at critically. I find it helpful to think of the physiological, psychological and social dimensions:

Physiological	Psychological	Social
1. Sleep	1. Addiction	1. Trolls and cyber-bullying
2. Unexpected, but common developmental problems	2. Gaming	2. Fake news
	3. Emotional problems (see Chapter 7).	3. Pornography (see Chapter 5)
	4. Obesity (see Chapter 6)	4. Privacy/Safety
		5. Selfies

SCREENS AND SLEEP

Herb: It's claimed that one hour a day on the screen will completely upset individual sleeping patterns. Canadian researchers attempting to find out why so few young people sleep up to eight hours have discovered that social media are, in general, the culprits. People who spend at least 60 minutes on WhatsApp, Facebook, Snapchat were the worst sufferers. They found that girls were more addicted than boys and most likely to be sleep-deprived in consequence.

Tony: We know that sleep deprivation leads to poor performance in school, and indeed is seen as an increasing concern, but it also leads to social difficulties and ultimately to mental health problems. It becomes a vicious circle. The more deprived of sleep an individual is, the less likely he or she is to take exercise physically and intellectually. What is the current received wisdom about young people and their sleep needs?

Herb: Advice varies, but in the USA, Canada and the UK, guidelines generally agree that young people up to 13 should have approximately 9 to 11 hours of sleep a night; those age 14 upwards should have at least 9, and when they are over 18 they should not have less than 7 hours of sleep in order to facilitate mental as well as overall physical health.

Tony: To parents, it sometimes seems as if waking up a teenager is the main challenge, but that is generally a healthy sign. Not sleeping is a more worrying trend. One study reveals that well over half of boys and two-thirds of girls have insufficient sleep.

Herb: The main reasons tend to be a lack of house rules, drinking coffee or popular, spiked drinks (the so-called energy drinks). Also, drinking alcohol or stimulating the senses before trying to sleep, by listening to loud music, for example.

BLUE LIGHT

Tony: Stimulating the senses also refers to the effect of artificial light. The phrase 'blue light' is often used in the context of impact on the brain, and must have an effect on sleep patterns.

Herb: We know that melatonin from the pineal gland regulates sleep and acts as light disappears, being secreted at its maximum at midnight and then gradually decreasing until light is back again. This, of course, was the pattern for early humans, who had no lighting apart from the occasional fires. We assume that they were mentally well insofar as their pattern of living allowed. Wakefulness and sleep were therefore fully predictable, and used appropriately. Not so nowadays. Blue light is emitted with intensity and efficiency by modern LED equipment, unlike the old-fashioned tungsten lighting, which had little impact on melatonin production. Blue light first became an issue in televisions, but with the advent of small screens being held ever closer to the eyes and the brain, it's far more significant. There are supposedly apps which decrease the amount of blue light emitted, but I am not at all sure how effective they are.

Tony: To an adult, this may make sense intuitively, but this kind of argument tends to be dismissed when talking with teenagers.

Herb: There is a telling, recent Swiss study which tracked sleepiness and alertness in boys aged between 15 and 17, some of whom wore glasses with filters blocking blue light, others clear glasses that did not. Those wearing filters slept far better than those who didn't, establishing the fact that melatonin production is more greatly affected by blue light in young people.

Tony: You are saying it really is the case that blue light affects young people significantly more than adults.

Herb: Yes. As things stand, far too many people (including adults) have the habit of going to sleep with their mobile phones in the bedroom. I would strongly advocate removing mobile phones not only from the immediate vicinity of a bed at night, but out of the bedroom altogether. It follows that the blue light screens emit should be turned off at least an hour before bedtime.

Tony: It's easy to understand why we love the colour blue, which is associated with relaxation, sky, sea and a general feeling of well-being. It also seems to govern circadian rhythms.

Herb: Yes, but blue is not a feature of the night, even though younger people are more sensitive to it. It's a kind of clock-setting mechanism which starts working when natural production of daylight isn't happening.

Tony: You don't need medical knowledge to see the effect of sleep deprivation. In school the impact is clear, in terms of the ability to concentrate on work, but also in the effect on relationships.

Herb: Special filtering lenses, of the kind widely advertised, are not proven to be of any benefit. Large television and computers screens these days emit more blue light than their predecessors. However you look at it, removing blue light from the bedroom should be a given for every teenager.

SOME UNEXPECTED BUT COMMON DEVELOPMENTAL PROBLEMS

New research is published almost daily with some bearing on adolescent health. Some examples:

- Excessive use of smartphones reduces cognitive capacity even when turned off or not present in the room. When phones are removed from the bedroom, the brain is less likely to malfunction, rather like preventing a battery from running down.
- Smartphones issue enough radiation possibly to trigger loss of memory in teenagers, particularly in right-handed individuals. The closer the phone is held to the right side of the brain, the more impact the radiation is likely to have on its development.
- Early adolescents who spend more than 30 minutes at a time on smartphones have a tendency to develop cross eyes.

- TTT (teen tendonitis) can cause pain in the hands and wrists as well as the back and neck from regular texting at speed.
- Text neck and curvature of spines as the result of sitting badly occur because bone and joint formation is not complete.
- Skin allergies and dermatitis are caused by chemicals such as the chromium, cobalt and nickel contained in smartphones, and rapidly disappear when phone usage ceases.
- There are even suggestions that fertility levels in males might be decreased from faulty sperm production due to smartphone use.

Tony: Is there not a danger that these research papers, or rather the way they are reported in the press, fuel a kind of hysteria around adolescent health? Day by day these research papers seem to contradict each other and, anyway, the number of teenagers deeply affected must really be pretty small? I see some recent claims that there are no health risks at all from screen use.

Herb: Certainly some newspaper headlines can be dramatic and inflated, but the sheer weight of growing evidence demonstrates that there are legitimate concerns. If used inappropriately, smartphones can seriously damage your health long-term.

SCREEN ADDICTION

Herb: The 2018 report from Ofcom is little short of horrifying. Some 150,000 children (6 per cent) aged 12 to 15 spend most of their waking time at the weekend engaged in online activity. Even more striking, 5 per cent of children aged between three and four are online more than three hours a day. This doesn't suggest active parenting. Time spent online, increasing all the time, it seems, correlates very strongly with mental health issues. UCL have noted that teenage girls who frequently spend their waking hours on social media from age ten onwards develop greater emotional and social problems.

Tony: What started off as a relatively simple thing has grown into a multi-headed monster. The technology seems to be developing faster than our means to control it.

Herb: Part of the problem is vested interests. It's good that internet giants are now required to examine their roles in the creation of so many problems. There's a lot of money at stake here. I feel there should be a statutory health warning.

Tony: It seems clear society faces a significant issue around screen addiction. The best response from parents is to do their level best to create an atmosphere in which a healthy breadth of non-digital activity is a significant part of the mix, while expressing an interest in their child's digital enthusiasm. But that's a tall order, and many people need advice.

Herb: There are many new apps to help deal with addiction – using the results to combat the cause, in a similar way to nicotine patches! One example is an app called Thrive. It does a variety of things, including gathering data about the amount of time spent on other apps, and allowing self-imposed limits to be stored which will cut off after an agreed time. It can be geared to suppress incoming calls. The message is, 'Just wait a bit and I will probably get back to you': it buys time. All such aids, however, require willingness on the part of the individual to exercise self-discipline.

Tony: We've already touched on this, and it's important. There is little doubt that, no matter how much parents try, most young people will be able to outwit them in terms of using their phones, whether at night in bed or popping out for a few moments. Whatever the attempts to limit or ban smartphones, they'll find a way round it. I come across plenty of examples of well-brought-up children in loving families who see no issue at all in deliberately tricking their parents. Normal family standards of ethical behaviour aren't necessarily seen to translate to the virtual world.

Herb: I have friends with teenage sons who have been addicted to their phones. All threats and sanctions were to no avail. Mother purchased a small safe into which the phones were placed immediately on return from school. Returning unexpectedly early one afternoon, she found both boys on their phones. Eventually she discovered a tiny camera in the corner of the room recording her use of the combination lock. That says it all! There are now apps designed to help parents. OurPact, for example, offers teenagers a choice: either use your phone the way we want you to, or we will confiscate it altogether. Even then this is not an easy proposition, as teenagers have to agree to having the app installed, and may yet find ways round it.

Tony: The answer has to be through education. Young people have to understand properly the ramifications of what they are doing, not in a heavy-handed or dictatorial way, but by exercising their own common sense and judgement. There's perhaps a parallel with what has happened with teenage smoking. ASH (Action on Smoking and Health) note that the largest decrease in smoking is in the 18- to 24-year-old age group: a consequence of more and better information being made available to them. They have to understand the broader context of mental health and well-being. So, too, with screens.

Herb: It's a question of balance, and parents need to remind themselves of that. Setting a positive example is a good first step. Not far off half of all parents, mothers more than fathers, admit to some degree of smartphone addiction. In addition, there's the problem of risk. The UN has recently warned that parents may be putting their children in danger by posting images and videos of them online, particularly so with younger children. Many parents video and take pictures of their children to what seems an obsessional level, regarding this as a harmless and pleasurable pastime. One teenager actually sued her parents in 2016 in order to have childhood pictures removed from Facebook on the grounds that they were violating her privacy.

Tony: Respect for others is an issue, whether for a child or other adults. I hear of cases where children complain, with some justification, that their parents are ignoring them because of the time they spend on smartphones. Being in the same room or vehicle, or anywhere else with a child, whilst one or other or both parents are on the phone is worse than being apart: it might reasonably be interpreted as a form of rejection. If a parent is capable of initiating a phone call without comment in the middle of a formal meeting with their headteacher (which has happened to me), there seems little chance they will be valuing time with their children. Apart from anything else, this is bad manners. Apparently there is now a new term for this: *technoference*.

Herb: I would go further. I think these are signs of parental neglect. It is claimed that over 85 per cent of adults in the UK own a smartphone, as do over 90 per cent of people aged 13+. There's a kind of social stigma attached to those not connected to the smartphone world. Use is pervasive – crossing the road, driving, cycling, at home, work, everywhere. It's the norm, even when illegal in some circumstances. Neglect comes if adults appear to be unresponsive and apparently uncaring when young people attempt to interact: it can be very damaging to the formation of relationships and the ability to develop social skills. Admittedly, it's hard not to respond to the demand of a phone attracting your attention. Indeed, some studies have determined that the 'dopamine high' from iPhone responses is almost equivalent to that of having sex!

Tony: On the other hand, smartphones are great for ease and immediacy of positive social contact. The issue, as ever, is agreeing acceptable boundaries within the family. These will not be identical in every case, but must be definite and emphatic.

Herb: It's helpful to remind ourselves how those individuals most connected with the arrival and propagation of the web have dealt with their own families. Steve Jobs, the founder of Apple, ensured that his children limited use of technology in his own home. Bill Gates and his wife did much the same. On a bigger canvas, Chamath Palihapityia, a former vice-president of Facebook, claimed that short-term dopamine-driven feedback was destroying the workings of society, through misinformation, mistruth, lack of co-operation and lack of civil discourse. What does that tell us?

Tony: Part of the problem seems to be an underlying fear people have that they're missing something. Indeed, this fear now has its own acronym: FOMO (fear of missing out). I've seen teenagers experiencing something like an acute panic attack when their smartphone support system has been removed. It must be similar to the severe withdrawal symptoms that can sometimes arise when ceasing to take a drug.

Herb: It is indeed a 'drug', and the scale of its impact is significant. Digital Awareness UK surveyed 5,000 students in England and noted that 56 per cent of them claimed to feel on the edge of addiction. They felt less confident about their lives generally and their appearance, too. A Swedish survey of nearly 12,000 students in 11 European countries noted that 4.4 per cent were pathological internet users. In Britain, the figure has risen to nearly 20 per cent, and rising. A Stanford lecturer has commented that 'For new behaviours really to take hold, they must occur often.' That is what is actually happening, not just in the Western world, but worldwide, as more than 3.5 billion people are said to be online.

Tony: Usually when we talk about addictions we mean substance abuse – drugs and alcohol in particular. An obsession with screens seems a lesser thing. Is this a true addiction?

Herb: It certainly is. The features are similar, and include: withdrawal symptoms if offline; constantly thinking about the tablet or computer; being increasingly restless and unhappy if attempts are made to stop over-use; not telling the truth about the extent of involvement; seeing usage as essential to relaxation; repeatedly being online more than originally intended; and becoming increasingly depressed or anxious when the device is not to hand.

Tony: The received wisdom seems to be that the best way to cut back on excessive use of the internet is by a process of gradual withdrawal. From my observation, this is one of those crisp pieces of advice that doesn't even get close to the difficulties lying underneath. Withdrawal symptoms themselves can be distressing – anxiety, lack of focus, loss of interest in other things and so on.

Herb: It can work if there is a system of staged rewards. A better route is often to enlist the help of friends or family who are similarly afflicted, and do so in a friendly, competitive way – for example, by agreeing a reward for whoever is best able to achieve the goals that have been set together. Honesty is crucial here. It means keeping an accurate diary, with a meeting every three or four days to check a precise record of how frequently they switched on, and for how long and in what setting. This only works for those who genuinely feel they are trapped in a habit pattern from which they cannot escape. In any event, the only people who successfully detox themselves are those who are truly motivated and recognize the extent to which their lives have been altered by their addiction, always unfavourably. It's undeniably hard, but it is quite possible to see someone gradually removing themselves from something which had become incredibly tantalizing and irresistible. The parallels with cigarettes, drugs and alcohol are only too obvious.

A CASE STUDY

When Father brought a computer home from work, his son rapidly became hooked. Because of the pleasure it gave him, parents bought him a small desktop for his 15th birthday. Bad move! Without anyone really noticing it, he missed meals, skipped classes, gave up sports and clubs, and withdrew from his friends. The family doctor suggested removal of the computer, which led to major rows and violence, including breakages, refusing bedtimes and meals, while crying constantly and claiming that his parents no longer loved or understood him.

Mother decided that the lesser of two evils was to return the computer. Unsurprisingly, behaviour worsened dramatically: on the machine 22 hours a day, eating sparingly from the fridge at night and ignoring personal hygiene completely. He was an urgent admission to the adolescent unit, dragged in kicking and screaming, uttering dire threats to his despairing parents, who needed immediate support in their own right. He was kept in the secure unit with no outside contact, and reluctantly started attempting classes. He had no computer access whatsoever at first. This was gradually introduced under supervision, alongside intensive psychotherapy sessions.

Eventually, daily leave to the family was agreed on condition that computers were locked away. The parents found this difficult, but persisted. After two weeks of progress he was moved to the open section with overnight stays at home, and was discharged on a trial basis ten days later. He knew instant readmission would follow if unsuccessful. Intensive family work was required, with computers kept under lock and key. The boy fairly happily resumed his former activities. Following some hiccups, the overall assessment six weeks later was encouraging.

The need for special camps, farms and units seems to be the best treatment option for such dramatically addictive, all-encompassing habits.

GAMING (SEE CHAPTER 8)
EMOTIONAL PROBLEMS (SEE CHAPTER 7)
OBESITY (SEE CHAPTER 6)

CYBER-BULLYING AND TROLLING

Tony: Poison-pen letters have been with us since antiquity. As a headmaster, I would occasionally receive anonymous letters criticizing something or other I had done or hadn't done. I found there was a simple expedient for dealing with such letters: the bin. In the electronic age that rather satisfying response can't have the same effect, because even a deletion is still there somewhere in the ether. Cyber-bullying and trolling are the two names used to describe unwanted attention online, particularly in relation to schoolchildren, and the terms are often used synonymously, but they're different.

Herb: Basically, trolls do their best to attract online communities in an attempt to feed their own attention-seeking and possibly even psychopathic characteristics. They often are narcissistic, self-interested individuals with seriously low self-esteem, elements of sadism and an overwhelming need to feel powerful. They leave controversial comments online in a general sense that can be racist, sexist and hateful, essentially to be as annoying as possible, while making sure their own anonymity is totally protected.

Tony: I remember in the early days of trolling, a convicted troll turned out to be a middle-aged woman with a family: not what I had expected at all. It seems we all have a propensity to hurt lurking in us.

Herb: I hope and trust that is not altogether the case, but it's certainly true that trolls will be found within all ages, ethnic groups and social classes. Trolling is not necessarily always vicious. A variant is Omegle trolling, which means having a video chat with random strangers, something which can go virtually anywhere. On the whole, trolls don't necessarily wish to offend, though of course they frequently do.

Tony: I suppose that might be somebody's view of a harmless way to pass the time, but it frequently turns nasty. I become very concerned when it impacts the lives of the young. Cyber-bullies are sometimes described as worse than trolls, a step up – because bullies want to hurt their victims, whereas trolls just want the attention. Yet trolls can be just as dangerous.

Herb: I see either group as similar to that most feared of all offenders, the arsonist. He or she has feelings of omnipotence, has no means of controlling the extent of the action once started, and takes great delight in being able to observe some of the effects. Anonymity increases the thrill factor: they can act innocent, or even be helpful if the victim is distraught.

Tony: Almost everyone I've met who deals with trolls professionally advises ignoring rather than engaging the individual concerned: starve of oxygen and let it die. With cyber-bullying, however, we are dealing with a different set of relationships which can be deeply corrosive and long-lasting. For schools, it can prove to be one of the most difficult issues to deal with. These can be slippery, intractable situations with high passions aroused on every side.

Herb: Cyber-bullies certainly are different, and tend to target an individual in order to produce the maximum emotional pain. They have a need to intimidate, humiliate, threaten, offend and cause as much distress as possible. This gives them the kick of empowerment without responsibility.

Tony: It's thought around one-fifth or more of children are now being bullied online, but the truth is not really known, and the figure is probably much higher.

Herb: Most people would probably cite child exploitation and grooming as the greatest threat from the internet. It is notable that Ofcom, in conjunction with regulators from other countries, places trolling, bullying and sexting as one of four main areas that require particular protection (together with extremism, risky actions and fake news).

Tony: We know we're dealing with a really significant issue, but it's hard to grasp and it can be taxing for schools and parents to recognize the signs of this insidious attack.

Herb: The anti-bullying charity Kidscape suggests that signs include: a reluctance to go to school without giving a reason; obvious withdrawal and unhappiness; extreme moodiness; unwillingness to switch off the computer or device at night; hypochondriasis without any features; and a sudden change in personality and ways of functioning. A number of the signs are generic, in the sense that they might apply to any bullying, but it is a fact of modern living that any form of bullying is likely to have a cyber dimension to it.

Tony: There's a striking number of ways in which people can use platforms for bullying. Often the platform was created with the best of intentions. For example, an app called Sarahah ('Honesty' in Arabic) was designed to create a kind of freedom wall for leaving messages. It has been abandoned by Google and Apple despite reaching over 300 million users. Misuse of the app led to several suicides. The advent of the cyber world has created a new mindset. I visited a top UK company years ago which saw virtue in putting up whiteboards throughout their head office departments, on which any employee was encouraged to write any comment about the company. The walls were conspicuously blank. In a physical space there was no guarantee of anonymity, so no one would chance it: the cyber world gives the illusion of complete protection.

Herb: Useful advice from Dr McLaughlin in Australia, who has noted eight different ways in which bullying can manifest itself. These are: hurtful trolling; flaming (aggressive comments); stalking (making it plain that the bully knows all the movements of the victim); exclusion (excluding someone from an online group, which could include gaming, teams or anything of that kind); fishing (falsification of online identity to establish romantic relationships); personalization (using the victim's name and account to damage them); threatening violence; and visual behaviours (posting pictures or videos in order to cause embarrassment).

Tony: Some people will always find new ways to hurt others. Good advice to parents is that they should contact the school if they have any concerns, just as the school should contact them. The people running good schools always want to have concerns aired with them, so there's a chance to do something constructive about the situation. I'm afraid that too often some parents will shy away from any contact at all, and others will storm in with a one-dimensional and completely unrealistic expectation that everything will be sorted out in a matter of minutes. Being targeted has a dramatic effect on self-image and self-esteem, and it's often very difficult for a young person to appear to be weak and ask for help. More often than not, parents will be reluctant to raise the matter for fear of making things worse.

Herb: Acting as a team to include the victim provides enormous emotional support and a strengthening of resolve and ability to cope. Let's not forget the inescapable fact that the bully has needs as well: it's easier to be anonymous than challenge someone face-to-face. Both bullies and victims are probably equally desperate people, but they're not always easy to detect and help. In cases of cyber-bullying, the perpetrators are clearly anxious, depressed and have significant self-image difficulties. That might not be the face they present to the outside world.

Tony: As practical advice, it's important for those on the receiving end of cyber-bullying to block the bully online, not to respond (probably not possible anyway, because most bullying is anonymous), keep records and, as far as possible, change the settings which permitted the torment in the first place.

FAKE NEWS

Tony: According to a group of British MPs, fake news is creating a potential crisis for democracy. Their particular focus is on the capacity for election results to be manipulated by foreign groups or even governments, but the issue ranges far wider. Communities and societies thrive if they're based on trust, a trust that has to be nurtured every day. Both the deliberate creation of false material (disinformation) and the unwitting presentation of wrong material (misinformation) undermine relationships right through society if they become a deeply ingrained habit. A headline scandal, such as Cambridge Analytica, where the personal data of millions of people were harvested and used without their knowledge in an attempt to predict voting outcomes, graphically illustrates how quickly a situation can run out of control.

Herb: It certainly does have a very negative effect. At a simpler level, fake news generated by minor incidents or even non-events can be very damaging. Teenagers in particular can be buffeted and confused by a blast of images and misinformation. The way teenage life is presented online is a version of fake news. To an average teenager everyone pictured on Instagram looks happy and glamorous, so they feel they're not the same, which can lead to profound feelings of failure.

Tony: There seems to be some kind of human predisposition to be attracted to the fake rather than the real.

Herb: It's now known that false news is much more exciting to create or redistribute than something which is clearly true. Genuine fact doesn't have the same power. A recent study at the Massachusetts Institute of Technology noted the difference in how true and false news items were tweeted and spread worldwide. They examined 126,000 stories between 2006 (when Twitter began) and 2017, involving 4.5 million tweets by 3 million people. Fake news was 70 per cent more likely to be re-tweeted.

Tony: I can understand the impulse many people would feel to pass on dramatic-sounding information: we all like to feel 'in the know', but I'm still not clear why people seem to be drawn to the fake. Maybe it's simply that fake stories are more dramatic and titillating.

Herb: I think that must largely be the case. The MIT researchers referred to 'rumour cascades', and concluded that falsehoods diffused significantly further, faster, deeper and more broadly in all categories of information, especially when related to political events. Platforms like Facebook, WhatsApp, Gmail, Instagram and Snapchat can all be used to peddle falsehood. The recent focus on Facebook and misuse of personal data only touches the tip of a very large iceberg, involving social media companies driven by the profit motive. As Mark Twain observed more than a century ago, 'A lie travels half way around the globe before the truth gets its boots on.'

Tony: In some respects teenagers are more savvy than adults: in school they can often see through to the truth of a situation with more clarity than teachers. For example, decades ago, there was a debate about the negative influence of comics on young people. The teaching profession among others were concerned that stylized violence would be mimicked. But teenagers themselves, the research of the time suggested, could actually distinguish easily between stylized fakeness and real-life behaviour. Teenagers are not guileless victims. However, the current situation is different in two respects: first, there is the sheer volume of material bombarding young people day and night; and secondly, any information can be presented as coming from impeccably credible sources – nothing stylized about it.

Herb: It's claimed that just 2 per cent of those under 16 are able to spot fake news. In the UK, a parliamentary group report states that 'It is driving a culture of fear and uncertainty amongst young people.' Perhaps oddly, younger children are more readily able to detect fake stories. Those from disadvantaged backgrounds, especially boys, who may have literacy problems as well, are the worst-affected, and may well be easily led astray.

Tony: A key element here is the quality of parenting. Children who are more likely to discuss problems with their parents generally develop critical skills of a higher order. Schools have a significant role to play, too. Developing critical skills should be absolutely at the centre of the school curriculum. Academic expertise, however sophisticated, is not much use if you can't see the wood for the trees. We run the risk of creating a generation of well-educated, gullible adults.

Herb: So what is the advice to parents?

Tony: I would ask my child's school to explain exactly how they develop effective critical skills across the entire curriculum. In particular, I would want to know that the issue of fake news is being tackled directly. It can also be useful to refer to agencies now working in this area. The National Literary Trust, for example, offers advice on how to teach children reasonable questioning and the concept of trustworthiness. Frauds and fakes have always been part of human history, and will continue to be, but a healthy degree of scepticism is a good sign. The underlying advice is simple: stop and think when you hear about something; ask yourself what the author is expecting people to believe; find out who wrote the story, and check whether it makes reference to credible sources (websites like fullfact.org can be useful); and learn to be honest with yourself – how does this story make me feel, and what does that say about me?

Herb: Another dimension is extremism. A recent report by the Policy Exchange has noted that the UK is the fifth-largest audience for extremist material online. Yet the internet providers wail about civil liberties when asked to remove dangerous material from websites. Being able to draw a fine line between being a platform-provider (with no moral responsibility) and a publisher (with some accountability) seems to me to be playing a dangerous game. These platform-providers have been described by one government minister as 'ruthless profiteers'. And there is a direct effect on young people.

Tony: Terrorist extremism may involve relatively small numbers, but underlying it is something that affects all young people. It's the way in which opinions are formed and become entrenched through the internet. Many studies have shown that once an opinion is formed about pretty much anything, it's very difficult to see another point of view, or even tolerate arguments which go against the grain. The classic case was in the 1950s, when it was the heaviest smokers who disbelieved the new evidence that smoking harms health. A constant and overwhelming flood of information tends to make us hunker down into our beliefs. What makes it worse is the culture of algorithms, which creates an echo chamber: if you believe X, then you are likely to believe Y, and the internet will provide it. The initial vision of the World Wide Web was to widen horizons and bring people together. Ironically, the internet is more likely to be the vehicle which separates us and puts blinkers on our eyes.

Herb: And this is at its most acute with young people, in whom the faculties of scrutiny, scepticism and entertaining openness have not yet been fully developed. Hence their susceptibility to repeated advertisements which initially might have been mocked or seen as ridiculous but eventually are accepted as a norm. I believe it's only a matter of time before governments take the decision to ban all smartphones and tablets from schools for children under the age of, say, 15. The French have done it already.

Tony: I fear that blanket bans don't help educate young people. And we need better education about the digital world, which we will touch on in Chapter 10.

PORNOGRAPHY (SEE CHAPTER 5)

PRIVACY/SAFETY

Herb: The largest technology companies have not been quite as good as they would like us to believe at confidentiality and controlling the content they are spreading worldwide. They are now on the defensive, and rightly so, but the dissemination of information will continue to grow, and it's only a matter of time before Sensurround virtual reality will control much of what we do, even if we tell ourselves we are still in charge.

Tony: It seems that there's not just a continuing growth in information, but a growth in the ways our privacy can be compromised. Surveillance Self Defence notes some of these ways: mobile signal tracking; international mobile subscriber identity (IMSI), which makes fake calls in order to gain information on individuals; wi-fi and Bluetooth tracking, where specific addresses can be captured even if the device is neither transmitting nor connected to a particular network; the fake blank screen, when the phone might appear to be switched off but can be continuing to monitor conversations and calls; 'burner phones', which are used briefly then discarded, in order to avoid surveillance; malware to infect phones . . . and the list goes on and on. It feels like science fiction is becoming reality.

Herb: As we grow older we tend to become more self-protective, and sensitive to areas in our lives that are potentially harmful. Teenagers have yet to develop effective impulse control, balanced judgement and feelings of empathy. They are the most vulnerable to all these invasions of privacy. As a general rule, individuals are not as guarded online as they are face-to face. Random and fleeting ideas can be enshrined permanently in the ether. Private expressions online can be an everlasting, haunting presence. We have seen enough personalities being vilified for something put out thoughtlessly on social media years before.

Tony: I've found it one of the most difficult messages to convey to teenagers: that nothing is ever anonymous online. Teenagers can appreciate the privacy point intellectually, but somehow it doesn't apply to them – until it does, and painfully. It may seem an uphill task, but that should not dissuade parents, teachers and peers from hammering home the message. One of the most effective ways I've seen is teenagers being shown in real time how their identities can be hacked and manipulated. We all need to see it to believe it. Young people need to know that knowledge is power, but unwittingly giving knowledge to other people makes them vulnerable and weak.

SEXTING

Tony: Another area of vulnerability is what is now called 'sexting', which generally means sending photos of a sexual nature by text. Ease of access and the smokescreen of anonymity can prompt both boys and girls to send images of themselves they will subsequently have cause to regret. I recall the case of a 14-year-old boy who sent images of his own genitalia to a girlfriend of the same age. The text was intercepted by the girl's mother. She immediately reported the incident to the police and, to the considerable surprise of both families, the matter was treated as potentially criminal under sexual harassment and grooming laws. In effect, the 14-year-old boy was regarded as an adult offender. In situations like this, one hopes common sense prevails: 14-year-olds have a habit of making mistakes which don't in themselves indicate any deep-rooted tendency or threat for the future, but it illustrates how robust the legal process can be.

Herb: Receiving or forwarding images or messages of a sexually explicit nature may seem relatively trivial for teenagers, but the fact is that sending such images by whatever means to others is regarded as a pornographic offence in most countries. In the USA, sexually explicit porn is illegal under the age of 18 even if self-produced. Teenagers have no idea of the appalling impact this can have on families when the information is widely revealed.

Tony: The point is that most teenagers and their families are unaware of the ramifications of sexting. Unaware in the sense that they may not have thought about the ensuing bullying, isolation, loss of reputation and negative self-image – sometimes even leading to depression and suicide. Unaware, too, of the serious legal difficulties teenagers can face.

Herb: It's interesting that the Girlguiding charity has noted that a third of girls aged between 11 and 21 state that their biggest concern online is having to compare themselves with the lives of others, which appeared to be perfect in every respect and which they could not emulate. Fewer than half of the girls felt that their parents recognized the pressures they were under, and two-thirds said their parents seemed to worry only about grooming. Online grooming is indeed an issue, but it is striking that parents as a whole tend focus on that, without appreciating the pressures young people are subjected to by the whole online experience. How could they? This is a new and constantly evolving technological world.

SELFIES

Tony: It's perhaps less significant, but the same might be said of selfies, too. Selfie culture is now pervasive: even prime ministers are seen taking photographs of themselves at public events. It seems a harmless enough thing – as indeed it is, in the main – but I've heard that a condition called 'Selfitis' has now been recognized as a genuine psychological problem.

Herb: This is the compulsion to place multiple pictures of oneself on social media. It is a self-destructive phenomenon. The intention is to post images that others will respond to in a flattering light. If only . . . ! There are seen to be three levels of Selfitis, reflecting the depth of engagement with confidence, acceptance, attention and competition. It can be overwhelming, requiring persistent validation, and could possibly fall easily under the umbrella of a body dysmorphic disorder, BDD (see Chapter 6).

Tony: Yet it's an acceptable social activity. In 2013 'selfie' was named word of the year by the *Oxford English Dictionary*, having been coined in 2002. I read that something like 4 million selfies are uploaded every day to social media across the world. I can readily see that concentrating too much on oneself can lead to impoverished relationships with other people, but is there a deeper psychological damage?

Herb: The inculcation of narcissism is one issue, but there's more. Although individuals don't always realize it, selfies are open to Photoshopping, which is widely used by celebrities to give a false impression of what they really look like – abdominals, breasts, buttocks, facial features and so on. Selfies seem to be simple and honest images, but they can lie. How easy to become emotionally destroyed by not appearing to be the way one would like to be in a fantasy version of the real. And these images are out there for ever. Loss of self-esteem, anxiety, depression can easily be the end result, with social isolation almost inevitable if done to excess.

THE NORMALCY OF SCREENS

Tony: Making reference frequently to a screen is now a normal, accepted and essential part of life. We have commented on some of the wonderful opportunities this technology presents, but also considerable problems and dangers.

Herb: Instead of the healthy interactions of to-ing and fro-ing in speech, connectivity, face-to-face contact and so on, children grow up unhealthily influenced by the one-way flow from the screen to the brain: receiving but not giving. This is the root of it. It might well be that state regulation and laws of various kinds will have to be passed to prevent this ticking time bomb from inflicting the damage it is so obviously causing at all levels of society and, indeed, at all ages. Again and again, we have to ask ourselves whether the negatives outweigh the positives, knowing full well that instant information is such a valuable phenomenon. Most adults can remember surviving and thriving in a world of magazines, books, lectures and conversations. We don't have to allow the dominance of social media in our lives to become an inescapable fact.

Tony: I'm not disheartened. There's some evidence that the tide is turning, that usage for many people has peaked and many young people are now taking more experiences in the real world. As has been noticed with the shifting demographic of Facebook, once older people take up something new it becomes a lot less attractive to the young. It's quite possible that a subsequent generation of teenagers might look rather pityingly at their elders' dependence on social media.

Herb: The fact remains that the internet is essentially a digital disconnect towards a false reality, and the problem we are facing is how to get the balance right. Where has good old boredom gone? It led to deeper thinking and exploration of new and original ideas, none of which came from a one-way interaction on a screen.

Tony: The digital world enhances our lives, but I readily accept that it also offers snake oil. The internet can be compensation for an inability to get on with real people, or a means to hide behind untested ideas in the belief that the rest of the world is wrong. It offers a fantasy existence leading to a brittle satisfaction with life. The balance you speak of can only come through openness, and regular conversation about the benefits and perils of the online world, from parents, teachers and, crucially, from peers. I have seen this very well done – it is possible. You and I would both agree that, taken as a whole, the opportunities and advantages of the online world are wonderful. The problems really kick in when it's allowed to be a private, shadowy, secretive place.

10

A Glimpse of the Future

It's a commonplace nowadays that we stand on the cusp of momentous change. The world our young will inherit is likely to look very different indeed from the world their parents understand. The change has already begun.

Artificial intelligence is rapidly developing. Super intelligence (ASI) is on the horizon, when the machine world will take over many human functions and not only do them more effectively, but also do things humans can't. The wonder of a machine programmed to beat a human chess genius, as Deep Blue did to Garry Kasparov in 1997, now seems ancient history. ASI will transform our world far more radically than the Industrial Revolution. It's the sheer pace of change that's startling – and frightening. The pundits argue that the age of ASI will bring us either incredible gifts, such as the eradication of disease and hunger, or the destruction of humankind. It will be a time of great risk and great opportunity. These twin themes are well known to anyone discussing adolescence: it's as though thousands of years of our development as a species have just about brought us to the point of our collective adolescence.

Human beings are linear creatures. We progress our thinking, develop our values and run our lives step-by step in what is, mostly, an ordered way. The changes we are about to face are not linear, but exponential.

In truth, no one really knows what will happen, or when, but it seems clear that children currently in school are beginning to contend with a dramatically changed landscape in which many of the familiar contours of inherited wisdom and experience simply aren't there. This has serious implications for the way we educate our children at school and at home.

There's an argument that schools will become redundant – we will be able to access better-quality teaching more cheaply online. But in fact the rise of AI, bringing with it the potential for children to learn without the need physically to attend school, only illuminates its real purpose which has always been fundamentally social. Being alongside other children, we learn better what it means to be human. Good habits begin at primary school level, supported at home, shaping personality to value self-control, motivation and work. This shaping needs the predictable structure of a school setting, offering routines and also a range of relationships that can't be achieved solely at home.

AI may eventually replace many things we do – calculations, repetitions, a great deal of analysis, precision – but this enables us to concentrate on the elements that truly differentiate us as human beings. At the heart of this are care and compassion, human qualities that give identity to society and need to be encouraged and celebrated if we are to survive.

Curiosity and creativity are uniquely human, too. Our default thinking is convergent, valuing speed of response: we intuitively look for the easy, default route. Creativity sparks when the default position is bypassed. This is as likely to happen in maths as much as music or art, depending on how any subject or activity is approached. Adolescents are particularly good at being creative in off-beat ways, and we tend to knock it out of them by insisting on convergent thinking through an exam system which was created for another age. Many discoveries and inventions have stemmed from the ideas of non-conformists, which is why we should never lightly dismiss new ideas from the mouths of adolescents – these could be the pathway to great things!

Quirky individualism can be a good thing, but it can also lead to a myopic 'me first' habit. We are social animals, and normally at our best when working together. Collaboration is another particularly human trait and a necessary human skill.

International employers say they require two basic qualities: creativity and integrity. They regard academic competence as a useful starting-point, but not much more than that: there are any number of well qualified graduates they wouldn't employ. We gain a spurious reassurance from the apparent safety offered by qualifications, when what we need is the range of skills and qualities that will make for effective citizens of our new world and an interesting life.

Surveys reveal most schools are fixed in traditional ways of doing things, but are often hazy about the bigger purpose. The same is true of how we think: most of the time we are not as self-critical and adaptable as we might like to believe. The most successful institutions and companies over the long term are built on lasting values, but are self-critical and light-footed about change. We need to be like that as parents; our children, too.

Some things don't change: literacy and numeracy will continue to be the essential cornerstones. Maths is the best test of intellectual rigour, but it's inadequate reading skills that hamper the development of so many young people. Research by Oxford University Press in April 2018 shows that the situation is worsening. Forty per cent of eleven-year-old students now have vocabulary so limited that it is significantly affecting their overall learning. Part of this is attributed to the limited vocabulary required online. One of the greatest gifts for any child is the intuitive habit of reading for the sake of it, best rooted at an early age, but still possible to achieve during adolescence.

A new element is digital education, not just in terms of technical skills, but helping young people feel confident and digitally aware. There is some good work in the field of digital intelligence. The DQ Institute programme identifies digital as just as important as intellectual and emotional intelligence. The programme starts with eight-year-olds and covers a range of issues aimed at producing 'wise, competent and responsible digital citizens' who use, control and create technology creatively for the benefit and well-being of self and society. The intention is wholly laudable. This is an area where parents can take direct action. Few schools at the moment run such a programme, but parents can access it.

In many ways this is a great age for young people: they are healthier and fitter than ever before, have the benefits of the internet age to stimulate curiosity and creativity, and the exciting prospect of tremendous advances for humankind in their lifetimes. Yet they also have to handle more complexity than past generations. This is one of the principal causes of teenage dissatisfaction and anxiety. Parents and schools can help by creating simplicity: having clear rules so that adolescents know where they are;

prioritizing the issues on which to make a stand; listening and explaining. If in doubt, keep it simple!

Now more than ever parents should be prepared to support and back their child's school, but equally be prepared to offer constructive criticism. Pupils should be actively engaged in the process. Adolescent and parent need to feel connected with education. It's extraordinary to think that not so long ago it was normal simply to direct pupils to the next task without them having any sense of why they were doing it. Adolescents, in particular, respond much better when they see the purpose behind what they are being asked to do.

At all stages, pushing academic aspirations to one side, however briefly, in order to take time off for other activities, is vital. Mental, emotional and physical growth are as important as everything else in development. This includes taking the stigma out of mental health problems, which can lead to empathy and a greater sensitivity to oneself and others.

It's easy to run off a list of the attributes today's adolescents will need to be effective in their futures – most people would cite, among others, adaptability, determination, values, confidence – but it's harder to say how these will be forged. A key is failure. Failure matters – it can lead to despair and giving up entirely; but failure is hugely valuable when it doesn't engender feelings of inferiority, but leads to the learning that breeds the habit of resilience. Schools and families should be places where failure is allowed and harnessed for better understanding.

So: what should we be teaching our adolescent children? Presented with the opportunity to devise the agenda for an international conference in South Korea in July 2018, a group of teenagers from different countries decided to focus on what mattered most to them. Their conference title was 'The Human Condition', and there were two principal themes: the impact of technology and social media on the lives of students, and how they could develop their emotional, physical and mental selves. They wanted to learn more about the science behind emotions, the effects of cyber-bullying, managing relationships within communities; they were concerned about healthy living, about the value of sport in developing self-esteem and about good and bad stress; and they wanted to discover more about how learning is most effective, about ethics in leadership and the value of meditation. They cut to the heart of it. Often teenagers have a clearer sense of what really matters than adults. Their chosen themes were relevant to their present and their future.

The education of the whole child is an idea as old as the hills, but has a fresh urgency for today's adolescents.

SEVEN ASPIRATIONS FOR ADOLESCENTS

By the time they reach the end of adolescence, we hope to see young people:

1 *Being comfortable in their own skin:* relaxed in the knowledge that identity is not fixed for ever. Personal uncertainty is all right, too. Having an ability to make confident judgements, not feeling pressurized by the expectations of others, and not rejecting whatever has been taught and shown out of hand. Feeling good about their strengths and achievements.

2 *Recognizing that it's not all about me:* able to feel empathy. Defining success not materially or personally, but genuinely celebrating the success of others. Having the sensitivity to appreciate that 'There but for the Grace of God go I.'

3 *Being able to seize opportunity:* approaching life with grounded optimism, able to face the uncertain and unknown with equanimity. Being positive-minded, both aspirational and inspirational.

4 *Celebrating creativity* in its many expressions, and wherever they may find it.

5 *Developing a nuanced sense of perspective:* seeing beyond the fake, and analysing arguments and expressing views in graduated terms. Knowing life never will be perfect or fair, and accepting that.

6 *Taking joy in true collaboration:* sharing ideas and taking pleasure in achieving a common goal.

7 *Seeing through the humbug of happiness:* knowing that it's not a target, but a by-product of what we do and the way we think. Being wary of unrealistic expectations of an ideal state of being; taking pleasure in the world around them and their part in it.

ACKNOWLEDGEMENTS

With our thanks in particular to Jane and Jenny. Also to all the adolescents who have enriched our lives.

And to the adolescent that lingers in all of us!

'The Child is Father of the Man'
William Wordsworth, 'My Heart Leaps Up' (1807)

'Live as long as you may, the first twenty years are the longest half of your life'
Robert Southey, *The Doctor* (1812)